CW00664130

GLOBAL ADVERTISING

Nükhet Vardar was born in İstanbul, Turkey, in 1961, and completed most of her education in Turkey. Subsequent to her university degree in Business Studies, she was at the University of Manchester, Institute of Science and Technology (UMIST) between 1983 and 1984, doing her MSc in International Marketing. After her MSc, she returned to Turkey and worked as a product manager at Turyag A.S. – Henkel's Turkish subsidiary – from 1985 to 1987. Encouraged by her work experience in a multinational company, she went back to UMIST in 1987 to work on her PhD, mainly looking at HQ involvement in the advertising activities of UK subsidiaries and UK advertising agencies. After receiving her PHD in 1989, she went back to her home country and was appointed as the Research and Planning Director of Yaratim/FCB – the Turkish partner of Publicis·FCB, Europe's second largest agency according to 1990 billings. Dr Vardar is currently working at Yaratim/FCB in İstanbul.

She enjoys writing, especially in the area of marketing and advertising. She has published, in English, articles based on her MSc and PhD. Her Turkish articles mainly appear in trade journals and dailies. Dr Vardar is a member of the European Society for Opinion and Marketing Research (ESOMAR), and the Turkish Market Researchers' Association.

GLOBAL ADVERTISING

RHYME OR REASON?

NÜKHET VARDAR
Research and Planning Director
Yaratim/FCB Advertising Agency

Paul Chapman Publishing Ltd
144 Liverpool Road
London
N1 1LA

British Library Cataloguing in Publication Data
Vardar, Nükhet
Global advertising: rhyme or reason?
I. Title
659.1068

ISBN 1–85396–143–4

Typeset by Setrite Typesetters Ltd, Hong Kong
Printed and bound by
The Cromwell Press Limited,
Broughton Gifford, Melksham, Wiltshire

To mom and dad
for their unconditional love
and never-ending sacrifices.

N.V.

CONTENTS

FOREWORD

> ... the most difficult part of globalisation was the reorganisation of the company. The problems encountered in internal organisation dominated all the others.

So writes Dr Nükhet Vardar, reporting the experience of one senior international marketing director of a major European multinational company. In many ways this blunt statement captures the theme and main conclusion of Dr Vardar's investigation into the practices of 'global advertising'. What emerges from her research is a picture in which the challenges remain those of *organisation* rather than strategy. For most practitioners, the task of defining *what* should be done continues to be somewhat easier than arranging *how* to make it happen.

Global Advertising: Rhyme or Reason? is concerned with the processes of managing advertising from the international perspective. It is essentially a book about management rather than about advertising. It does not deal, in any depth, with creativity or the craft skills of advertising execution. Rather, it explores the thinking and actions of those executives who create the environment in which such skills must be deployed.

It is a popular belief that a company's advertising activities are primarily shaped by reference to *external* factors, such as the wants and needs of consumers, and the demands of competitive differentiation. Dr Vardar's survey starkly illustrates that, in the international arena, one should not under-estimate the major influence of *internal* factors, such as established attitudes, structures and working relationships. Such internal factors often exert a disproportionate impact on the nature and extent of advertising harmonisation across countries.

The characters in Dr Vardar's 'story' are not the well-known 'gurus' of international marketing and advertising theory. They are the people at the day-to-day coal-face who are responsible for translating theory into practice. The main foundation of the book is a research survey conducted among agency executives, based primarily in London and responsible for international client business. In interpreting these findings, Dr Vardar draws upon a comprehensive knowledge of the existing literature on the subject. However, the core value of her work springs from this collation of views from a wide range of agencies and from all levels of agency management. This survey provides genuine, real-life insights into the practical challenges of managing advertising programmes at the international level.

The overwhelming impression is one of complexity and of international advertising plans that are 'easier said than done'. The reader becomes acutely conscious of the fine lines that exist between 'consensus management' and bland compromise; between 'co-operative flexibility' and deliberate ambiguity; and between strategic vision and the 'art of the possible'. Dr Vardar's book is, by definition, a survey of practices in the 1980s, but its usefulness lies in helping to prepare practitioners for the greater challenges of the 1990s. By providing a detailed picture of past pitfalls and successes, the book implicitly identifies opportunities for improvements in future practices.

Dr Vardar, wisely, offers no general all-purpose solution to the managerial challenges of international advertising. Indeed, one of the strongest themes emerging from the book is the need to tailor management systems to the particular requirements of individual brands and companies. These 'requirements' are a combination of market-place considerations *and* the specific organisational capability of each company and its advertising agency. Plans, however worthy, remain only plans if the structures do not exist to make them a reality.

Dr Vardar's survey and conclusions are entirely her own and are not subject to the influence of the present writer. However, it is impossible to resist the temptation to close these opening remarks with some observations of my own. These will be brief.

It is clear that this is a subject in which there can be no 'rules' or formulae for success. However, I believe there are some *principles* with universal application:

1. Objectives for the management of advertising at the international level should be set in precise and specific terms:

   - It is essential to distinguish between a management process that seeks to explore the appropriate level of advertising commonality between countries, and the preconceived determination to standardise advertising across countries. The former process is increasingly mandatory for all significant companies, whereas the latter approach will prove a blind alley for all but a minority of businesses and brands.
   - The 1990s will not see a major proliferation of standardised 'global advertising' – rather a substantial growth in the effective international management of brand positionings/advertising strategies and the opportunistic transfer of great ideas across borders. Objectives should be stated precisely in these terms, rather than in the previous 'ambiguous' jargon of 'global advertising'.

2. National effectiveness is a higher priority than international 'tidiness' or cost-efficiency:

   - The best international advertising strategies will not compensate for loss of touch with local market-places. There are still too many examples of international advertising initiatives motivated almost exclusively by the desire to reduce the cost of advertising development and production.
   - Such initiatives are 'penny-wise and pound-foolish'. Advertising development and production costs are a relatively small proportion of the total investment made in strong brands. Scale economies in these costs are false economies if they reduce the effectiveness of national media spending, damage brand equity and demotivate local management. All of these considerations should come higher on the list of priorities than efficiencies in the cost of advertising development/production.

3. Committees are not renowned for their creativity:

   - The difference between a mediocre ad and a great campaign is essentially the relevant application of creative skills. Creativity is not some mystical preserve of a department of an advertising agency. It is *the* fundamental component of effective advertising at both the local and international level.
   - Steering committees and consensus management are often important elements of multinational co-operation. While such groups may be useful in securing agreement on strategy, they typically stifle creativity. Wherever possible, the responsibility for creative development in international advertising programmes should be delegated to a 'lead market', and made the responsibility of a single client executive. Ideas that cross borders spring from creative processes exactly similar to those that have lead to outstanding national campaigns.

So, in summary, there are three key principles: set objectives in unambiguous terms; acknowledge the priority of national effectiveness; and avoid committee management of creative processes. These principles will not guarantee success but at least they may provide clear sign-posts charting a way through the rough seas of international 'complications'.

Global Advertising: Rhyme or Reason? closes with Dr Vardar's wish [that] this book will be seen as a stepping-stone in the area of global advertising . . .'. I, too, hope that the book will fulfil this role. There are exciting and rewarding opportunities in the 1990s for those who successfully apply the lessons of the 1980s.

Les Naylor
Director of Client Services
Young & Rubicam, Europe

PREFACE

After being engaged in the rigorous activity of thesis writing for six long, long, months, where the use of titles, subtitles, subsubtitles and big words were very common, my publisher challenged me with just the opposite. He said, 'If you think you know what you are talking about, you should be able to say it in plain English and it should still make sense to the practitioners of the business'. (He was too polite to say it in so many words, but his words were to the same effect.) This was the right push to give me sufficient motivation: I decided it was time to share my research with others, and that I was not going to let the lonely experience of doing a PhD be filed as a 'wasted experience'.

Following this decision I had to make up my mind about the style of the book. I had this bundle of research findings, but the word that pops into most people's minds at the mention of the word 'research' is 'yuk': research is considered to be anything but stimulating and fun. I did not want to put the reader off, so I avoided jargon, statistical analytical results and my mathematical model. However, I did not want to write the book for the sole purpose of being entertaining and lively. If I had done so, readers would feel they were being given anecdotes or allowed to peep through someone's diary. After first marking the no-go areas, I was left with only one alternative.

Doing research was never a rose garden for me, and I doubt if it ever were for anyone. The times I found most rewarding while conducting this research were the ones when I was amused and actually entertained by the findings: I have tried to convey that state of mind and mood in the book, in the hope of capturing the reader's interest. I believe strongly that research does not need to be boring or a cure for insomnia – my aim was to convince the reader of that. I hope you will spare one or two smiles and a few laughs while sailing through the pages of this book while, at the same time, reading cured (but not raw!) and fresh research findings. I have to add that this book has no resemblance to my actual PhD. Although it is derived from it, it does not include any quantitative analyses conducted on 399 international brands marketed in the UK, which form a substantial section in the thesis. In other words, the results obtained from clients are left out. Furthermore, the writing style adopted has been totally altered: it is now less formal and more colloquial. The contents pages and the headings used were made entirely unrecognisable, because the book is aimed at practitioners in the advertising world. Even so, and even though the book differs vastly from my PhD, I wish to thank Dr S. J. Paliwoda, who was my supervisor throughout my PhD years.

I am solely to blame for any omissions or mistakes in this book: I apologise for them in advance. Needless to say, these were not intentional. Although I take entire responsibility for any shortcomings, I have also to share any credit the book might receive with others. This book would not have been published if I had not had the support and collaboration of numerous helpers. First of all, I have to thank the agency executives who agreed to allow me interviews, and who spared their precious time over them. Although a few chose to remain anonymous, I extend my heart-felt thanks to them all for sharing with me their vast experiences and honest views on global advertising. This most definitely gave me a different perspective in tackling the problem. I have to thank twice those executives who granted me permission to name them, their accounts and agencies, individually in the book. I believe it makes the reading much easier, and the book livelier and more authentic.

In addition, I wish to thank the Manchester Business School Librarian, D. Ross, for helping me to update my figures, and Shirley Taylor, of the Department of Trade and Industry, for sending me a copy of the latest broadcasting directive. I am grateful to them not so much for sending me the information I desperately needed, but for proving that dependable and responsible human beings have not totally become extinct from the face of the earth. I am also truly indebted to Asuman Ökten for faultlessly word-processing the manuscript, as well as for making life much easier for me during the writing-up process: her help aided in rubbing off all the horrifying experiences I had had in the past. I am also grateful to Les Naylor for agreeing to write the Foreword for the book. Although we have not met, I heard a great deal about him during my agency visits and also from reading. It is therefore a great honour to have a foreword written by him.

My publisher, Paul Chapman, deserves much more than just plain thanks: I am grateful to him for putting his trust in me. It was his initiative that turned the inconceivable into this book. We somehow managed to communicate across the whole of Europe without major cut-offs. This book is, therefore, a definite example of the successful transfer of information across borders! Having now finished the manuscript, I genuinely hope that his entrepreneurial spirit will pay back exponentially in the near future.

Dr Nükhet Vardar
İzmir
May 1990

1
GETTING STARTED

The title of this book asks that there be rhyme or reason in global advertising. Its main theme, therefore, is that, in most of the previously published sources, the concept of global advertising is tackled in an over-simplified fashion. From a distance, global advertising is generally (and mistakenly) found very attractive – mainly because it looks a simple, quick and cost-effective exercise. However, once agencies and clients find themselves participating in global advertising, they face other, more complex issues. A lack of local management support, agency commissions, local-authority/local-responsibility dilemmas and chaotic agency–client relationships, for instance, become common place. Such problematic issues suddenly become visible and, needless to say, they are very intricate matters and very tricky to cope with. When these problems occur, global advertising immediately loses its attractiveness. This book aims to address these issues and to highlight the less-known and less-talked-about side of the global advertising debate. In all, practising global advertising successfully is not an easy task and should not be taken lightly.

Alternatively, the move towards a single market in 1992, and the drastic political, economic, cultural and fiscal changes that are taking place in the USSR, the Republic of China and East European countries, all indicate that global advertising is here to stay. These recent developments undoubtedly also exert additional forces, making successful global advertising practice essential. Therefore, in the light of these changes, agencies and advertisers need to be fully equipped to be able to meet the challenges set by global advertising. As a result, this book also aims to guide both international agency executives and marketing executives towards securing smoother relationships with each other while running successful international campaigns; it demonstrates that better agency–client relationships give rise to successful global campaign transfers, which will play an even more crucial role after 1992. It therefore makes practical recommendations to both account and marketing executives. And it is believed that these can be applied to real-life situations.

The book is aimed mainly at advertising and marketing practitioners. As it is concerned with the successful practice of global advertising, it will appeal to readers from both international advertising agencies and multinational companies. It is hoped that professional agency executives (with such responsibilities as account executive, account director, account supervisor, international co-ordinator, regional account co-ordinator or director) will find it of value. Similarly, on the client side, it will be relevant to product (brand) managers, group product managers, marketing managers, marketing directors and, to a lesser extent, to sales managers. In addition, as a specialised book, academic researchers in the future, working in the area of international advertising and marketing, should find it helpful. It will keep them in touch with the latest state-of-the-art in international advertising. It will also aid them by helping them to build on already-conducted research and to justify their own research aims.

The main body of the book is devoted to reporting interviews conducted with agency executives of international advertising agencies in their London offices. Direct quotations taken from these face-to-face interviews are used abundantly throughout. The focus of these individual interviews was to identify those certain preconditions that formed the basis of a smooth transfer of international advertising campaigns across borders. The information referred to in this book is derived from 39 international accounts, which resulted from personal contacts with 33 agency executives in 13 international advertising agencies' London branches. Information was gathered through 36 personal interviews and 3 postal questionnaires. The study of agency executives was part of a larger-scale piece of research, which covered 399 product managers of international brands marketed in the UK by foreign-owned multinational corporations (MNCs). The findings from clients are not reported here. However, the suggestions and recommendations made look at global advertising from the broader perspective of both agencies and clients. In a nutshell, the book concentrates on information obtained from agencies on international accounts for ensuring the smooth transfer of international advertising campaigns across countries. It has been written with the firm belief that it has something new to say, and that it says this with the help of lively and, at times, humorous quotations taken from the personal interviews with agency executives.

The agency executives who were interviewed were later contacted by a letter, which asked for their permission to include direct quotations from their interviews. Before sending this letter, it was confirmed that the executives were still at the same addresses. For those who had moved, the letter was either addressed to their new business or their successors were contacted for permission. Apart from one negative reaction, all the executives were co-operative, helpful and even excited about the idea of turning this series of interviews into a book. Few wished to remain anonymous; others wanted to make amendments before giving their consent. Four months after the first letter, a reminder was sent to those who failed to reply, which added that it was assumed that their permission was given if there was no response within a reasonable period of time.

Before reviewing what is covered in each chapter, a few points regarding the terminology used in the book should first be clarified. For the sake of simplicity and differentiation, the term headquarters (HQ) is used when referring to clients' HQs, whereas the term head office (HO) is used for advertising agencies. In addition, the words 'international' and 'global' are used interchangeably, as is discussed in Chapter 2.

Chapters 2–4 outline the current state of the global advertising debate, including concepts, diverse views and some statistics. Chapter 2 is devoted to a preview of the basic concepts used in the book: definitions of international advertising, advertising objectives, models that help in measuring advertising objectives and what is meant by 'successful' advertising. The views of advocates and opponents of global advertising are discussed in Chapter 3. Based on the views of both, the reasons why advertising cannot be standardised are summarised in a table at the end of this chapter. Chapter 4 opens with some figures on UK and world advertising expenditures. The factors that heighten the importance of advertising in today's world are noted. Future trends in international advertising, such as the new media and the single-market concept in Europe, are discussed in Chapter 4.

Chapter 5 looks into HQ involvement in international advertising. As the research was on HO/HQ involvement in the advertising activities of international advertising agencies, standardisation of marketing, products, promotions and advertising campaigns across countries are reviewed. The shortcomings of previous research are also highlighted. The current issues raised are listed at the end of Chapter 5.

The findings obtained as a result of the interviews are reported in Chapters 6–9. Chapter 6 deals mainly with the agency–client paradox, the core of their relationship and the agency HO's role in this. Chapter 7 concentrates on the organisational structure adopted by international advertising agencies while running global campaigns, emphasising the client's influence in the adopted structure. Two separate agency HOs are also identified – one actual and one official. A distinction is made among different bodies found within agency organisations, such as the regional (European) HOs and the UK agency. Chapter 7 proves how agencies actually 'mirror' their client's organisation within their own while running international campaigns.

Chapter 8 looks at agency executives and how they feel about global campaigns. Advertising types suitable for global campaigns, according to these executives, are listed. In addition, definitions of 'successful' advertising given by the executives interviewed are summarised. Also, the relevant degrees of standardisation in global campaigns that each individual element of marketing mix is subject to are reported.

Chapter 9 starts on a high note, claiming that 'Your campaign has the right to be global, too'! The question of 'how' is then tackled. Three different approaches used by agencies are explained in detail, and examples are given of the co-ordination or creation of global campaigns. Links between global campaign development and clients' corporate cultures are established. Hence, by identifying the corporate culture of each client, the agencies can actually decide on the correct co-ordination method for campaign development on that particular account. Finally, the extent of adaptations made in the UK for global campaigns, and the campaign elements adapted, are discussed. Agency executives' speculations regarding the near-future impact of satellite TV on global advertising are noted.

Chapter 10 gives an overview of the findings detailed in Chapters 6–9. These are concluding remarks, mainly summing up what has been said on each subtopic. This chapter also includes suggestions for further research topics in global advertising. Gaps found in international advertising are pointed out. Finally, this chapter includes a thirty-itemed agency checklist, devised as a pragmatic tool for assessing the suitability of accounts for global campaigns. It is derived from the entire body of the research findings.

Appendix I explains how the research was conducted, how the agencies were selected and how they were contacted. It concentrates mainly on the research methodology used without going into too much detail. Appendix II includes the two questionnaires used while collecting the information from the agencies. The first questionnaire was used in personally administered interviews, and the second is the postal version of the same questionnaire.

It seems we have a long journey to cover. Let us embark for the mystical land of global advertising and try to unveil its secrets. The motto will be 'rhyme or reason' throughout the journey.

Bon voyage.

2
ADVERTISING – A TRICKY TERM

FROM DEFINITION TO DIVERSITY

Advertising is a tricky term mainly because it uses words that have no meaning unless they are filled with meaning. Advertisers consider words to be triggers and, obviously, they aim to choose words that trigger positive images, feelings and thoughts – though it is never as simple as that when it actually comes down to doing it. Agency people spend sleepless nights trying to find the way through the wild jungle of words and different languages to the minds of potential consumers.

As advertising and marketing practitioners are well aware, this is not the sum of all their problems: one other major hurdle is over-communication in today's world. This is a problem all free societies face. If you want to be effective, your message should be over-simplified to communicate to the over-exposed mind. But we cannot ignore communication altogether simply because there is too much of it in the market-place, and this problem is actually at the root of the dilemma. The effect of communications has become even greater in an era of over-communication (1).

The problems do not cease after the advertising has been communicated. Advertising can be easily acknowledged without being persuasive, in which case the advertising efforts will be a total waste. Advertising should attempt to persuade people to try a product and to continue to use it after the trial.

It is no secret to anyone in advertising or marketing that advertising decision-making means working with many unknowns and under uncertainty. The target is the consumer, but there is no direct personal contact with the consumer – no immediate feedback is available. The allocated space and time is limited: in a few seconds it should deliver a message in an intelligible form. It should also follow a logical sequence (2). There should be a general predominant theme in all campaigns.

As if to make things worse for practitioners, it is not possible to find a single and a simple definition of advertising. Ogilvy believes that advertising is not a form of entertainment or art, but a medium of information (3). Others emphasise that it is not a science, and that it should never become one: 'It is best treated as a dynamic, creative experience always open to the open mind – a constant challenge in mass salesmanship in persuading potential customers to buy and to "outstrategize" competitors' (4, p. 63).

Russell and Verrill (5, p. 23) give an honest account of advertising, indicating that 'Advertising is persuasive communication. It is not neutral, it is not unbiased; it says "I am going to try to sell you a product or an idea". In many respects, it is the most honest and frank type of propaganda'. These definitions enhance different but integrated facets of advertising.

Diversity in advertising is therefore not only limited to the challenges faced or the problems encountered: there is also diversity in its definitions. Overall, consensus is hard to find in this field, and it is probably this characteristic that makes it an exciting, highly envied and very competitive area. There are no set patterns to follow; rather, those who emerge with new patterns hold the key to the rose garden of success.

ANOTHER MINEFIELD – INTERNATIONAL ADVERTISING

The seeds of debate on international advertising have been sown since the 1960s, following the rise of multinational corporations (MNCs) throughout the world. International advertising is defined as the practice of standardising, integrating and transferring types of advertising across countries, without taking country-specific differences into account.

Usually, international brands are located somewhere on the decentralised–centralised continuum, ranging from 'decentralised multidomestic' to 'global' brands. J. McCann, of the McCann-Erickson Agency, expresses the agency's belief that the global brand is advertised in ten or more countries, and marketed by multinational and global clients who are located somewhere on the world-brand continuum (6). Global advertising does not mean one single campaign running around the globe – it simply indicates that there should not be one campaign for every market (7).

Before going any further, it is necessary to explain certain terminology. As far as concepts go, international and multinational advertising do not mean the same thing. In international advertising, campaigns are run in many countries but they are controlled from the advertiser's HQ. In multinational advertising, local campaigns are produced in many countries. The campaigns could be the same or different. However, the crucial factor is that the subsidiary country spends more time with multinational advertising.

Although it is accepted here that international and multinational advertising mean different things, 'international' and 'global' advertising are used interchangeably in this book for advertising campaigns used in a number of countries that keep the same theme but that modify slightly their execution in local markets.

WHAT'S THE BIG DEAL IN INTERNATIONAL ADVERTISING?

International advertising is a complex process mainly because it involves numerous and various parties, and because it extends over borders. As soon as someone spells out 'international advertising', they need at least to put company HQs, company subsidiaries, agency head offices (HOs) and local agency branches into the picture at once. As a result, communication networks become more tangled and more delayed.

However, MNCs often feel that, to be complete, a well-co-ordinated international management needs a uniform advertising concept across subsidiaries. This should be able to combine international management principles with local flexibility. These requirements demand sophisticated services from international advertising agencies. In addition, clients' HQs need to give full support, and local subsidiaries have to provide total collaboration while practising international advertising. With all these conditions to be fulfilled, no wonder it proves to be such a complex task! Why, then, do advertisers become involved in international advertising in the first place?

MNCs mainly feel compelled to make this co-ordination of management work because of their competitors and because of the fierce market conditions of the 1990s. Companies talk about 'chances of survival', 'defensive and offensive strategies', 'marketing warfare' and the like. All these analogies remind one of military tactics and campaigns. The MNCs' main target is to be able to meet the demands of the 1990s. MNCs hold the firm belief that the only way of reaching this target is through tackling the business globally; otherwise, they do not give themselves much chance of surviving the slaughter of international competition (8, 9).

As was pointed out by one of the agency executives interviewed by the author (Chapter 8), MNCs are influenced and, in return, influence each other to a great extent. They see their own chances of survival as very slim (let alone winning the battle) unless they are organised in the same global manner as their competitors. As one of the interviewees put it, 'It is almost like a religious concept. There is only one God and that is global marketing'.

Therefore, when MNCs vehemently support international marketing, believing that their survival depends on it, the importance they assign to international advertising increases proportionately. However, the difficulties of establishing and maintaining this delicate equilibrium called 'international advertising' stay with them throughout. It should be remembered that international advertising is considered, at the heart of the struggle, as the marketers' most significant and controllable weapon (4).

WHY SET ADVERTISING OBJECTIVES IF YOU DON'T MEASURE THEM?

Setting and measuring advertising objectives are other areas of controversy in this subject. Objectives are necessary if we want to know whether or not we have achieved our set targets at the end of advertising campaigns. It is also said that 'good performance may occasionally occur in the absence of objectives, but it can rarely be sustained' (2). No doubt, if advertising objectives are properly defined, they increase communication efficiency. Having aims to work towards also resolves possible conflicts with the HQs. Advertising objectives are usually considered to be the main link between subsidiaries and their HQs throughout the year. They also serve as performance measures or benchmarks following the completion of advertising activities (4).

However, advertisers and agencies sometimes overlook setting advertising objectives or they become so involved in the advertising itself that measuring performance against predetermined objectives is forgone. Then 'advertising for advertising itself' becomes the priority. Obviously, the whole point of advertising is to make the product or the service the hero. The positive effects of advertising should be visible in sales, in market shares, in improved image, in increased awareness or in any other preset advertising objective – whatever that may be. There are many examples of off-targeted advertising. These advertisements are a great success and gain high credibility, but they fail to help the advertisers in reaching their targets (10).

Advertising objectives, therefore, should be realistic and in line with marketing objectives, working towards the same end; they should be attainable within the allocated budget; they should be functioning as a control measure for HQs in evaluating subsidiary performance; and they should be measurable. In short, these objectives operate as communication and co-ordination devices. They provide criteria for decision-making, they evaluate results and they work as a measure of advertising performance. Advertising objectives need to be precise and there should not be too many of them, otherwise multiple objectives will mean multiple targets. Ultimately, the campaign ends up being a 'compromise campaign', not fulfilling any of the objectives if there were multiple objectives to begin with.

In other words, advertising objectives should be exact and specific. Once advertising campaigns are over, they should be referred to and performance should be checked against them. Otherwise, why waste time setting them in the first place? Interestingly, the *New Collins Dictionary* (1985) defines the word 'campaign' when used in a military context as 'a number of operations aimed at achieving a single objective'. Thus, the popular analogy accepted among advertisers that draws similarities between international business practices and militaristic activities should also extend to the definition of a 'campaign'!

TOOLS AND OBJECTIVES

Tools are necessary if objectives are to be measured. Not surprisingly, tools devised to measure the effectiveness of advertising against predetermined advertising objectives are as numerous as objectives themselves. Without going into detail, two models will be mentioned here, one formulated by an academic and one by a practitioner.

The first model is called DAGMAR I (Defining Advertising Goals for Measured Advertising Results) and it was developed in 1961 by R. H. Colley, a well-known academic (11). It aims to plan advertising by selecting and quantifying goals. Performance is measured against these goals at a later stage. The major trap to avoid in this model is not to mix advertising objectives with marketing objectives. Although marketing and advertising objectives need to be complementary, they are not the same thing: marketing objectives are broader and very general, and generalities are always more difficult to measure.

The marketing people at the advertiser firms should be the ones who specify the advertising objectives for any particular campaign. They should have access to related data made available to them by their market-research departments. Marketing people should concern themselves with what to say in the ad to benefit their brand and leave the saying of it to their agencies – they should define goals, not write copy.

Once advertising objectives have been stated, the specific communication task to be performed by that particular advertising campaign is defined. These objectives act as a benchmark: at a later stage, progress or performance is measured against them. If they are not measurable, then the marketing people's judgement will play a crucial role in assessing the effectiveness of the advertising.

This model is also known by different names, such as the Hierarchy-of-Effects model or Advertising Force model (2, 12). It basically consists of the following steps:

Unawareness → Awareness → Comprehension → Conviction → Action

The ultimate goal is to bring about buying action, but moving consumers up the levels of communication also indicates advertising effectiveness.

The second model is known as the FCB Grid. It was developed in co-operation with Professor B. Ratchford of New York State University to be used in the Foote Cone & Belding (FCB) Agency (13). In this grid, awareness and knowledge are grouped under 'learn'; liking and preference as 'feel' and conviction and purchase as 'do'. The FCB Grid is shown in Table 2.1.

The model has four quadrants: 'Think', 'Feel', 'High involvement' and 'Low involvement'. 'Think' and 'Feel' are not on a continuum, they are related to the same product. In different countries, the same products tend to be grouped in the same quadrant, so this model is, therefore, especially attractive to MNCs. It implies that the mental process consumers go through when choosing a product is the same across countries. This grid is very useful in developing

Table 2.1 The FCB Grid

	Think	Feel
	Economic	Psychological
High involvement	Learn → Feel → Do	Feel → Learn → Do
	Responsive	Social
Low involvement	Do → Learn → Feel	Do → Feel → Learn

(*Source:* Reference 13.)

the correct advertising, after it has been determined where the product is situated on it. In low-involvement purchases, consumers may purchase first before changing their attitude. In this case, 'do' comes before either 'learn' or 'feel'. For such products, advertising will not be informative. Hence, in high- and low-involvement products, different advertising strategies need to be used (14). Today the general trend is to move towards the right-hand side of the grid, mainly because products and marketing techniques are becoming globalised, and advertising din is increasing. The FCB Grid is detailed and has the flexibility to accommodate the different characteristics of products.

There are other widely known tools, such as CAPP (Continuous Advertising Planning Programme), which was developed by the Leo Burnett Advertising Agency (15). More recently, another technique, known as 4Cs (Cross-Cultural Consumer Characterisation) was developed in the USA in collaboration with the Young & Rubicam (Y & R) Agency. This is basically another psychographic grouping. When the author contacted an account planner from Y & R in July 1987, Y & R (London) was using 4Cs. Published sources also confirm that Y & R is planning to extend the use of 4Cs in France and Holland (16). Other cross-cultural consumer research has been conducted over the years to understand consumers more fully and to create more effective advertising directed to these subconsumer groups. Studies on life-styles (17), benefit segmentation (18), activities, interests, opinions (AIO) (19), values and life-styles (VALS) (20) and on psychographics all aim to understand the consumer and the consumer's needs better, mainly because consumers with different social characteristics respond dissimilarly to different advertising styles (21).

Advertisers and agencies need to be careful when choosing the right tool for measuring their advertising campaign's performance. The abundance of these tools makes the selection difficult and risky, because using a wrong tool is as bad as using no tool at all – if not worse!

'SUCCESSFUL ADS': ARE THERE ANY MIRACLE ADS?

Any discussion about setting and evaluating advertising objectives leads to an elusive and undefined concept: what is 'successful' advertising? This concept is neglected possibly because it *is* so difficult to define and measure. However, the whole point of setting objectives and of using models to measure advertising effectiveness is to identify successful ads. Corporates must utilise the information gathered and the experience gained from previous advertising campaigns. However, in order to be able to assess campaigns, predetermined advertising objectives should be available to check against them.

In successful campaigns, advertisers identify the problem, have well-aimed advertising goals and recognise a successful campaign when presented with one. In this book it is accepted that 'successful' advertising fulfils previously determined objectives set by marketing people as advertisers. In other words, once the campaign is over and the advertisers ask themselves, 'what did we accomplish?' and 'what did we want to accomplish?', the answers to both these questions should match (or at least come close to each other). The answers of agency executives interviewed by the author are included in Chapter 8. It is interesting to note which characteristics in a campaign receive top priority by advertisers when evaluating the success of a campaign.

At every mention of 'successful' advertising, advertisers and agencies find sales figures used as a measure of effective advertising. The use of sales figures for this purpose is usually a nightmare for the parties involved, mostly because advertising success depends on many other marketing and product-related factors, such as a satisfactory product, durable packaging, and a smooth distribution system for the brand. In addition, campaigns (good or bad) show their effect after a period of time. Therefore, examining sales figures during or just after the campaign would be to deny the 'lapse effect'.

Widely recognised criteria for measuring advertising success include giving information; receiving exposure; obtaining attention, recognition, readership, comprehensiveness, recall and credibility; creating motivation; persuasion; moving consumers up the communication ladder; and purchase and repurchases (22, 23, 24, 12). Advertising's effect is seen best at the recall of the brand at the purchase point. It is the effect that stays with the consumer, after screening and forgetfulness have taken place (24).

Although purchase and repurchases are included among the measures of successful advertising, they should be considered as complementary to the other measures mentioned. An increase in sales can be considered as a marketing objective. Marketing objectives are supposed to be general, but a growth in sales by leaps and bounds cannot be achieved solely through one single advertising campaign. The 'sales effect of advertising' is considered to be a far too limiting concept, taking as it does a restricted view of a complex process (25, 26, 27). Direct-response advertising is left out of this generalisation: the increase in sales can be measured in direct response (27). Glover (28) points out that sales can only be used as a measure if the product is at the growth or maturity stage in its life-cycle.

When measuring success, it is also important to decide which peer group's reaction is important. Should we be seeking consumers' reactions to a given ad as the target audience, or the agencies' as the creating bodies, or the advertisers' as sponsors? Who is in a better position to judge? Whose judgement is to be trusted? One piece of amusing research indicates that advertisements that were considered to be successful by agency executives were not liked by the consumers (29)!

To complicate matters even more when assessing advertising effectiveness, it is acknowledged that different methods for measuring advertising effectiveness are popular in different countries (30). While comparing the effectiveness of a campaign across countries is said to be difficult, imagine all the stumbling blocks to be faced while actually transferring an international advertising campaign across borders. These different aspects of a 'successful' ad suggest that there are no 'miracle' ads; rather, agencies and advertisers need miracles in order to come up with 'successful' campaigns!

In this chapter we have reviewed certain concepts that form the basis of international agency-client relationships: sound concepts secure sound relationships. It is even more helpful if agencies and clients mean the same things when they use these terms freely. As a starting-point, we wanted to be sure that readers understand what is meant by these frequently mentioned concepts. Now it is time to turn our attention to a meatier and more formidable subject: the burning issue of whether or not to globalise. The pros and cons are listed first, so that readers can decide what is best for themselves.

REFERENCES

1. Ries, A. and Trout, J. (1986) *Positioning: The Battle of the Mind*, McGraw-Hill Management Series, Maidenhead.
2. Aaker, D. A. and Myers, J. G. (1987) *Advertising Management* (3rd edn), Prentice-Hall, Englewood Cliffs, NJ.
3. Ogilvy, D. (1983) *Ogilvy on Advertising*, Pan Books, London.
4. Peebles, D. M. and Ryans, J. K. jr (1984) *Management of International Advertising – A Marketing Approach*, Allyn & Bacon, Boston, Mass.
5. Russell, T. and Verrill, G. (1986) *Otto Klepner's Advertising Procedure* (9th edn), Prentice-Hall, Englewood Cliffs, NJ.
6. Paskowski, M. (1984) A quartet of agencies tunes to separate global notes, *Marketing and Media Decisions*, December, pp. 43, 44, 130, 131.
7. Ritchie, R. (1986) Global branding need not mean global advertising, *ADMAP*, January, pp. 39–42.
8. Wieringa, S. (1989) Trends in world trade, *Flying Dutchman International 2*, Vol. 3, issue 2, pp. 16–19.
9. De Benedetti, C. (1987) Europe's new role in a global market, in A. J. Pierre (ed.) *A High Technology Gap?*, Council on Foreign Relations, New York, NY.
10. Citroen (1984) *Marketing*, Vol. 18, no. 9, 30 August, pp. 30–3.

11. Colley, R. H. (1961) *Defining Advertising Goals for Measured Advertising Results*, Association of National Advertisers, New York, NY.
12. Lavidge, R. J. and Steiner, G. A. (1961) A model for predictive measurements of advertising effectiveness, *Journal of Marketing*, Vol. 25, October, pp. 59–62.
13. Berger, D. (1986) Theory into practice: the FCB Grid, *European Research*, Vol. 14, no. 1, pp. 35–46.
14. Ray, M. L. (1973) A decision sequence analysis of developments in marketing communication, *Journal of Marketing*, Vol. 37, January, pp. 29–38.
15. Maloney, J. C. (1966) Attitude measurement and formation (paper presented at the Test Market Design and Measurement Workshop), AMA, Chicago, Ill., 21 April.
16. Kleinman, P. (1987) The research market, *ADMAP*, September, pp. 16–18.
17. Anderson, W. T. jr and Sharpe, L. K. (1971) The new marketplace: life style in revolution, *Business Horizons*, Vol. 14, pp. 43–50.
18. Haley, R. (1971) Beyond benefit segmentation, *Journal of Advertising Research*, Vol. 11, no. 4, August, pp. 3–8.
19. Wells, W. D. and Tigert, D. J. (1971) Activities, interests and opinions, *Journal of Advertising Research*, Vol. 11, no. 4, August, pp. 27–35.
20. Mitchell, A. (1983) Styles in American bullring, *Across the Board*, Vol. XX, no. 3, March, pp. 45–54.
21. Kassarjihan, H. H. (1965) Social character and differential preference for mass communication, *Journal of Marketing Research*, Vol. 2, May, pp. 146–53.
22. Aaker, D. A. and Day, G. S. (1986) *Marketing Research* (3rd edn), Wiley, New York, NY.
23. Longman, K. (1971) *Advertising*, Harcourt Brace Jovanovich, New York, NY.
24. Krugman, H. E. (1975) What makes advertising effective, *Harvard Business Review*, Vol. 53, no. 2, pp. 96–103.
25. King, S. (1977) Improving advertising decisions, *ADMAP*, April, pp. 164–73.
26. Worcester, R. (1987) Why communications count, *Management Today*, May, pp. 76–9.
27. Corkindale, D. R. and Kennedy, S. H. (1975) *Measuring the Effect of Advertising*, Gower, Aldershot.
28. Glover, D. R. (1976) Advertising effectiveness measurement: communication *vs.* sales revisited, in R. D. Michman and D. W. Jugenheimer (eds.) *Strategic Advertising Decisions: Selected Readings*, Grid Publications, Columbus, Ohio, pp. 319–27.
29. Lovell, M. and Potter, J. (1975) *Assessing the Effectiveness of Advertising*, Business Books, London.
30. Schwoerer, J. (1987) Measuring advertising effectiveness: emergence of an international standard?, *European Research*, Vol. 15, no. 1, pp. 40–51.

3
TO GLOBALISE OR NOT TO GLOBALISE: THE CURRENT STATE OF THE DEBATE

THE BEST THING SINCE SLICED BREAD

Supporters of international marketing and advertising often base their arguments on certain common perceived advantages. The most widely given reason for defending international advertising is that economies of scale are achieved in marketing expenditures – its use leads to savings in personnel and production costs. These, by return, are a substantial economy for the company, and the company can then supply better-quality goods to the consumers at lower prices.

Although the economy drive is an influential factor in deciding to use international campaigns, not many tangible examples are cited. Whenever the cost-savings issue arises, Heller's (1966) work is referred to (1, 2, 3). In Heller's example, the added cost of producing separate commercials for each market is estimated to be approximately $8 million annually. No other figures are given by multinational corporations (MNCs) to demonstrate the cost effectiveness of international advertising.

Other reasons given for defending international advertising are:

- As a result of these savings, larger budgets can be allocated to advertising and research and development (R & D). This would, in turn, make companies more competitive in the long run.
- Technological changes (such as the use of satellites in telecommunications and information technology) are taking place throughout the globe. These developments will bring about converging consumer needs.
- The influence of global media, such as the same TV series being shown extensively around the world, satellite TV, the international press and magazines. These also help to homogenise the tastes of world consumers.
- Media spill among neighbouring countries creates a cumulative, positive effect on consumers if the advertising message is uniform across countries

(small, central European countries are most often given as examples).

- The positive effects of uniform packaging and the advertising message for foreign travellers and migrant workers. This creates a consistent company image and guarantees standard product quality across countries.
- The increase in world travel leads to a standardisation of consumer wants: 'Almost everybody, everywhere wants all the things they have heard about, seen or expected' (4).
- Other often-repeated reasons for running international campaigns as a result of converging consumer needs include zero population growth in the Western world, higher living standards, the emancipation of women, fewer married couples, fewer children, and the erosion of the traditional family unit (5). However, non-Western countries (where population growth rates are so high they are expressed in percentages, not thousandths) should not be forgotten. Unfortunately, these countries account for more world consumers than those with a zero population growth rate.

Levitt (6), the international-marketing guru, claims that the 'republic of technology' is the binding factor in keeping consumers together. The 'republic of technology' consists of the 'proletarianisation' of three major forces – communications, transport and travel. By proletarianisation is meant widespread access to these forces, both economically and functionally. With converging consumer needs, a new set is said to emerge: the global set, replacing yesterday's jet set (7, p. 24):

> Global Set are numbered in millions. They are the most regular travellers among the 50 million passengers who use international air services each year. He is a male business traveller. He is aged 30 to 45, wears a Christian Dior shirt and tie, carries a Samsonite suitcase containing a bottle of duty free Black Label whisky, Dior or Hennes aftershave, Sony radio, Gold Cross pen, *Time* magazine, Amex Card and travellers cheques and a Canon camera . . .

The list goes on. The global set may be very influential, but it is not so when the total world population is considered. Less than 50 million people in the total world population of approximately 5,000 million account for less than 1% of the world's population. For the sake of 1% of world consumers, advertisers and agencies cannot turn their backs on the needs of the other 99%, can they?

In the execution of international campaigns, the most frequently repeated phrase is 'good ideas tend to have a universal appeal'. It is also acknowledged that good ideas are rare and hard to come up with. Once found, they should be exploited fully. MNCs and international agencies should be prepared to draw on the similarities in different countries and not to emphasise their differences (8, 9, 10). This generates managerial intensity and focus, and puts an end to the dilution of efforts: 'Globalisation means speed, aggressiveness and clarification of tasks for everyone' (11). Quicker product roll-outs are also mentioned in connection with the necessity of running international campaigns. With quicker product launches all around the world, there is no time to develop specific national campaigns (12).

In a nutshell, the promoters of international advertising preach the oft-quoted remark of Pepsi Cola's Chairman: 'One sight, one sound, one sell.' The view supporters adopt seems to over-simplify the entire process. The justifications for running international campaigns given so far are actually promoters' personal feelings and beliefs. In many cases they are backed up by anecdotal evidence. Ideas are not reinforced with the aid of research findings – or anything tangible, for that matter ... We will now look at what their rivals have to say when attacking international advertising.

FROM INTERNATIONAL ADVERTISING TO TRAGEDY

To support their views, opponents of international advertising stress the individual differences found in countries, pointing out the blunders that happen when marketers are ignorant and insensitive of these seemingly trivial country-specific variations. The common factor in all these blunders is a lack of market knowledge in any given situation, and striking examples of these can be found in a variety of published material (13–17). Kotler (a well-known academic) does not share Levitt's views on globalisation: he is quoted as saying that, if globalisation is considered seriously, then, in marketing terms, this means taking a step backwards, because globalisation stresses production rather than specific consumer needs (18).

The opponents of international advertising generally emphasise the differences across countries regarding language barriers (even in the regions of the same country), religion, tastes, culture, standards of living (discretionary income), the literacy rate, advertising legislation, media availability, distribution channels and a lack of international advertising agencies. It is also stressed that local execution should be the norm – not the other way around (19, 20).

Taking all these limitations into consideration, it is no wonder that companies that have accepted global marketing and advertising 100% are a rarity. The German company, Henkel, is cited as one of these rare exceptions (11). How they tackle this issue is outlined in the following quotation:

> They [Henkel] compared their markets to a highway that passes through a wide variety of terrain – some rocky, some sandy, some flat, some with peaks and valleys. So the highway is the same throughout, but the support structures are different depending on local circumstances. The variations between the support structures and settings of the highway are provided locally, but the direction of marketing comes from one source only.
>
> (*Ibid*. p. 42)

Another interesting comment that opposes international advertising was made by Harris (21). He points out that brands that have been marketed by international advertising are often cited as proof of the success of international advertising but, he says, no one can prove that these brands' success is actually a result of their commitment to global advertising.

Having raised some general points used in the argument against international advertising, we shall now look at the logic behind them. Interestingly, opponents often come up with their arguments by overthrowing the advantages listed by supporters.

Economies of Scale

It has been suggested, bluntly, that there is no scientific data to support the cost-savings aspect of international advertising for MNCs (22). In one study, where 27 companies were interviewed, only one produced documented evidence on the savings resulting from standardisation (23). It has also been stressed that cost reduction does not necessarily mean profit maximisation, especially in international marketing where the general rule is that achieving economies of scale is critical and difficult (24). In an agency, costs seem to go up in the short term as a result of doing business with international clients: O'Brien admitted in an interview that international clients are a new challenge for agencies, and hence take up more resources. He also added that 'if we stayed multidomestic, an advertising agency would have less expense' (4).

As to cost savings in advertising production, it was argued that amending internationally produced films to accord with local needs resulted in more expense (21). Amendments included changes because of different regulations; dubbing; shooting subtitles; and the pack shot. Additionally, the cost of advertising production is relatively low compared to the cost of buying advertising space and time. Therefore, wrong advertising can lead easily to a waste of the entire media budget. Harris (21) indicates that companies could be saving £25,000 or £40,000 per country. This appears to be a large sum of money but, if the ad is wrong, then the total losses in sales revenue could rapidly make such savings seem insignificant. Although economy drive often emerges as a seemingly sound argument used by supporters, once this argument is examined closely it becomes clear that economies of scale in production costs are not easy to achieve by either MNCs or agencies.

Converging Consumer Needs

There are today new consumption classes in the world: people previously inherited life-styles but now they choose them for themselves. People identify less with nations and more with groups, professions and subcultures. The developments taking place in communications technology have created new choices that encourage cultural divergence not convergence in consumer needs (25). The main argument put forward against converging consumer needs is that, whatever may happen, the consumer is *always* local. The following expresses this idea effectively (37, p. I): 'Everywhere there is a different consumer, modified by tides of social change that are sweeping the world. The rate of change varies, the nature of change varies; but change is the common denominator of international life'.

An executive of a large MNC is quoted as saying 'Why do I need eight different advertising campaigns in Europe? From a ten-foot pole in Brussels I can see all of Europe!' However, Peebles and Ryans (26) stress that geography and cultural life-styles are partially related. They advise MNCs to be ultra-sensitive towards the cultural differences observed, even in the adjacent countries of Europe.

This latter point leads to the concept of 'nationalism'. Nationalism is seen as an obstacle to the converging needs and tastes of world consumers, and it has proved to be counterproductive to the growth of the European market. Mexico, Canada, Australia and New Zealand have also been cited as experiencing an upsurge of nationalism in advertising (27, 28).

Laroche, addressing the American Marketing Association's Conference in Montreal in 1987, suggests that 'unlike the US, Canada does not aspire to become a "melting pot", but rather a "salad bowl", in which each ethnic group participates fully, but still retains its original identity' (29, p. 27). One recent example of nationalism comes from the four Scandinavian countries: SAS Airlines tried to promote the SAS language as these countries' common business language. However, it failed in its efforts because of the fierce national independence of the separate countries, even though no one could deny they have a great deal in common (30).

Increases in Foreign Travel

The number of tourists in a total population is small enough to be neglected. There is also the question of 'Are tourists exposed to local media during their stay and in a language they do not understand?' (21). In addition, taking Mintel figures for British tourists spending their holidays in foreign resorts, it is pointed out that only one fifth of the population is spending one twenty-fifth of its time in an overseas country – this is by no means a mass market.

Bernstein, a well-known adman, commenting on the international HQ function of co-ordination, says that this 'meant making sure that the logo and consumer promise were identical throughout the world so that the Yugoslav peasant on his next visit to Colombia would feel at home!' (31, p. 133). All these views emphasise that the role of the well-travelled consumer is exaggerated when listing the advantages of international advertising. In world markets, the global set is still restricted to a small minority. On the other hand, the mass market of consumers who do not belong to this global set spend very limited time in foreign markets, if they ever get a chance to travel abroad.

Translation/Transliteration

Translation and transliteration are other areas in international advertising that raise opponents' suspicions when a campaign is transferred across countries. The literal translation of creative copy is a minefield of potential linguistic disasters (even simple market-research questionnaires produce surprises). MNCs and agencies are warned about unqualified translators and direct translations. A consensus has now been reached on the importance and significance of transliteration as opposed to literal translation (32, 33).

Apart from words and their significance in advertising, the importance of non-verbal communication is also undeniable. Facial expressions, gestures, postures, glances, smiles, emblems, clothes, colours, spatial distances and vocal inflections are all clues that help people receive and send messages. These clues should not be ignored in an ad, otherwise it is labelled 'foreign' (17, 34).

Advertising Legislation

In the UK, two, main, self-regulatory bodies are concerned with advertising. One is the British Code of Advertising Practice (BCAP). This monitors press, magazine, outdoor and direct-mail advertising. The second is the Independent Broadcasting Authority (IBA). This administers the code for TV and radio commercials. It collaborates with the Independent Television Companies Association (ITCA) and with the Association of Independent Radio Contractors (AIRC). Restraints are self-imposed and self-regulating. However, the Advertising Standards Authority (ASA) provides an external check on the self-regulatory system. It ensures the system works in the public interest and its opinion on any matter concerning the interpretation of the code is final (35).

A further body helps in establishing links between UK advertising legislation and the outside world – the Institute of Practitioners in Advertising (IPA). The IPA has been acting as the industry body and professional institute for UK advertising agencies since 1927 (36). It modifies draft legislation frequently before it affects advertising. While doing this, it collaborates closely with the Advertising Association and the European Association of Advertising Agencies. It also tries to ensure that UK agencies' viewpoints are represented at Council of Europe discussions.

This is the position in the UK. However, different countries have different regulatory bodies and different advertising legislation. Illuminating country-specific examples are given by Dunn and Lorimor (37). Also, a detailed comparative analysis of voluntary regulation in the UK and the USA was conducted recently by Miracle and Nevett (38). It is, furthermore, widely known that the legal climate in Europe concerning advertising is changing rapidly. Globally, even very specific issues relating to advertising legislation are far from similar, for example, the use of foreign languages in advertising in Western and non-Western countries (39).

The differences in advertising legislation in different countries necessitate compulsory adaptations in global advertisements. There are, in the main, three distinct groups of countries that have their own individual approaches to advertisement regulation (40):

- Scandinavian countries apply a consumer-ombudsman approach.
- Anglo-Saxon countries rely on self-regulation.
- Developing countries emphasise the protection of their cultural identity.

As has already been pointed out, there are wide differences in advertising legislation among European countries, even among member states of the EEC. Needless to say, however, these differences will be ironed out by 1992, unless the single-market concept is doomed to linger on as a mere dream. The Council of Europe, therefore, feels compelled to work towards this unification: a draft directive prepared by the Council of Europe, Committee of Ministers, in Strasbourg (March 1989), and the Broadcasting Directive accepted in October 1989, are reviewed in Chapter 4.

Local Management Support

Moving too quickly and too far towards global marketing could cause problems at the local-management level; local managers could lose interest and enthusiasm. The 'not-invented-here' syndrome prevails in attitudes to advertising that has been imposed by HQ. Local management can ask for financial compensation for international advertising that has been thrust upon them. An example of this was the introduction of Henkel's product, Sista – a do-it-yourself sealant. After it had been introduced successfully in Germany, HQ in Düsseldorf insisted its launch in other European countries be carried out in the same manner. Local managers, however, only agreed to use the standardised advertising in their own countries on one condition: Düsseldorf would undertake the first year's advertising and promotion budget. Obviously, local managers wanted to reduce their own financial risks; they refused to allocate their limited budgets to something they did not believe in (41). Furthermore, if a company globalises too quickly, some good managers might leave the company or lose their motivation, as their total responsibility has been reduced overnight from one of establishing strategy simply to one of execution once HQs start to send ready-made advertising campaigns.

Another disadvantage in HQ involvement in advertising campaigns is that HQ slows the subsidiary down in its activities. If everything needs to be checked, approved, signed and sealed by HQ first then, by the time a decision is reached, it could be too late. Subsidiaries should not be tardy in responding to local market conditions – that is, if they want to retain their competitiveness.

G. von Briskorn, International Marketing Director of Henkel's adhesive products at the time, gave an example of Henkel's marketing approach when addressing a conference in London (42). According to von Briskorn, the most difficult part of globalisation was the reorganisation of the company. The problems encountered in internal organisation dominated all others. After a careful investigation, the early involvement of affiliates was encouraged. At this stage, HQ organised workshops and seminars. He concluded that any managers who did not accept these newly introduced rules were sacked. However, even this measure is not powerful enough to demonstrate the significance of local-management support in international advertising. If local managers will not side with international campaigns, then these campaigns do not stand much chance of success in their markets. In this case, either the local managers or the international campaign is sacrificed.

The following is taken from a magazine ad from the Ogilvy & Mather Agency (O & M). It reflects, probably, the feelings and ideas of all global-advertising challengers. It is also an effective review of what has been said on the subject so far. What's more, it says it all with such an elegance and style that it is almost lyrical. The theme of the ad is 'creating the Asian image – the cultural connection'. They are saying that O & M believes in ads that are culturally relevant, that connect the West to East. It reads as follows (43, p. 183):

> Many creative directors in Asia have perceived American advertising as the international form. The form that Asian advertising should derive from. It isn't. The best American advertising is pure Americana.
>
> The American experience is a potpourri of mostly European and African cultures with two centuries of pioneering spirit. This in no way resembles the fifty centuries of cultural depth in the Asian consumer. What is the significance of a Western jingle to a person who dances beautifully to the sound of a bamboo flute?
>
> It is an Asian Creative Director's responsibility to conceptualize, visualize and verbalize the Asian experience.
>
> In Thailand a rather notable experiment in making the cultural connection has been executed over the last seven years for a local beer called Singha. It is a film campaign in which we do two or three new productions each year. The refreshment benefit of the product is visualized and verbalized in a way that can only be described as ethnically Thai. Symbolically with the coming of the monsoons. Graphically in the heat of a bronze casting yard. Emotionally with the sound of Thai street vendors. The music tracks use only Thai instruments. Voice-overs are created in a Thai poetic style, which is literally untranslatable. Rich with detail, the commercials are usually slow paced and run sixty seconds.

Needless to say, the campaign was very successful. It received a number of Clio awards, not to mention a trebling of sales. O & M drew three lessons from this rather passionate campaign:

- Campaigns can be developed that speak successfully with an authentic Asian tongue.
- Not an inch of professionalism or style need be surrendered in so doing.
- This form provides more originality and vitality than a copy of any Western style.

The points raised in this chapter and the issues emphasised by both advocates and opponents of international advertising clearly show that the subject of international advertising is one of great disagreement. Unfortunately, the debate is based mainly on feelings and, at best, anecdotes – as the last two sections indicate. The time is now ripe, therefore, to turn our attention to the few studies that have been undertaken (I deliberately refrain from using the word 'research' so as not to discourage the reader), in the hope of shedding some light on the subject.

RECOGNISING THE STORM SIGNALS: WHY ADVERTISING CANNOT BE STANDARDISED

First, not many studies are available on international advertising, but the ones that are show that it is not possible in most cases to use standardised campaigns. If they were used, they could easily lead to detrimental consequences.

In the discussion that follows, previously conducted investigations on international advertising are grouped under seven headings. All but two emphasise that standardised advertising will not work (these exceptions are highlighted in Table 3.1). The seven groupings of investigation mainly concentrate on:

1. executives' perceptions of international advertising;
2. different consumer target-groups' perceptions of the same advertising campaign, which lead to different purchasing behaviour;
3. products that are less suitable and more suitable for advertising transfers;
4. differences in market readiness and market conditions;
5. differences in popular media across countries;
6. differences in how advertising messages are received across countries; and
7. differences in advertising styles in countries for achieving different results.

Each grouping looks at a different aspect of advertising. None the less, the general theme they all reflect is that stereotyped decision-making processes are not advisable. International marketers are warned about the manifold variations in different countries, cultures, advertising environments, product groups and customer groups for the content of their advertising, the advertising types preferred, the media used, and so on. They all emphasise that the issue of global advertising should be handled with the utmost care if mishaps are to be avoided. Keegan (2) states that the 'more you know about a country, the more you think it is unique'. This affirms that knowledge is power, and it puts an end to ignorance. Unless a particular country is studied in depth, nuances will go unnoticed. Unfortunately, however, hasty generalisations rule company executives' major international advertising decisions. Although everyone is aware of national differences, this awareness seems to be compounded of many half-truths (44).

Table 3.1 summarises the previous studies undertaken. These all display the reasons why advertising cannot be standardised, giving evidence from seven different but very interrelated areas of advertising. A quick reading of Table 3.1 gives one single message: the different examples relating to different product groups and services across the world suggest that there is a clearly felt need by corporates to differentiate their global campaigns over borders. These non-standardised, locally adapted campaigns must incur extra costs for the corporates. However, if their earnings did not exceed these added costs then they would simply not use non-uniform advertising. Is the cost factor (which is generally referred to as the major advantage of global advertising) actually then a fallacy? As tailor-made products were eventually produced at lower costs,

Table 3.1 An overview of storm signals – why advertising cannot be standardised

1. *Perceptions of executives*

- A comparison of business executives' attitudes about advertising in eight European countries and the USA. Europeans are more sympathetic than their US counterparts, except about advertising's effect on children. Differences emerge (45).
- A comparison of Harvard Graduate School's and Dunn and Yorke's (45) research on how executives perceive advertising. The pan-European approach does not seem likely (46).

2. *Perceptions of consumer target groups*

- A longitudinal study of US and German subscribers of product-test magazines. Less favourable attitudes in both countries over time, especially among younger age-groups. Differences between countries in various aspects from different economic and social dimensions (47).
- The attitudes of consumerists, students, academics and managers, about advertising across countries. The strongest differences exist between managers and consumerists, but no within-group differences emerge in regional subgroups (48).
- UK consumers' attitudes towards US and UK advertising. Successful US commercials are not effective in the UK (49).
- Life-styles in the UK, USA and France are compared. A comparison of grocery and fashion-purchase behaviour of US and French working wives belonging to different life-styles indicates that the 'traditional' role is still powerful; however, the definitions of liberal and conservative change from country to country (50).
- Cross-cultural life-style analyses on UK and US women show a rejection of traditional homebound duties by UK women. This warns marketers of this difference when planning their promotions, as it reflects on women's buying behaviour (51).
- A cross-cultural study on US, French, Indian and Brazilian students concludes that ads should contain different attributes from US ads, as purchasing criteria differ (52).
- A comparison of family decision-making roles in the USA and Venezuela finds changes in the roles of husbands and wives. Ads should consider the product-specific attitudes of consumers (53).
- An examination of consumer attitudes towards foreign products in different product groups concludes that ads should consider consumers' product-specific attitudes (54).
- The similarities regarding across-border consumers who have high incomes, a good education, white-collar work, interests in seeking information, low status concern, low conservatism and low dogmatism (55).
- A strong reaffirmation that segmenting customers according to their needs across borders ignores the differences in 'symbolic references' that are crucial for the success of the advertising (21).

3. *Product groups*

- The use of three models to analyse life-style data cross-nationally. The most productive one is identified as the product-specific profile to check the suitability of international advertising strategies (56).
- Different degrees of standardisation applied according to product groups. Cosmetics are more suitable for centralisation, whereas food needs to be decentralised (57).
- Brands with simple advertising propositions, that have a low-information content and that are low-involvement packaged goods, as well as products and services directly related to overseas travel or communication, are more suitable for global advertising (21).

Table 3.1 Continued.

- The global appproach accords best with low-priced, non-durable goods, that also fulfil basic needs (58).
- In the automobile, TV, camera and calculator industrial sectors, the calculator sector is identified as having the highest internationalisation in the development of its ad themes (59).
- International advertising requires favourable conditions with regard to the availability of the product, competitive country climate, consumer usage segmentation, advertising history, the advertiser's organisational structure and the available advertising package (60).
- A report on Clark's (1975) findings states that a higher degree of centralised leadership is possible and desirable with some types of products, particularly those that are not part of the indigenous socio-cultural background but are introduced from outside (61).
- In the low-tech world of packaged goods, brands with an essentially functional appeal may be more successful in a global approach (62).
- World brands benefit from standardised advertising if they are ubiquitous and universal in appeal, they are consumed for the same basic reasons, their similarities outweigh their differences and they have consistent and long-term positioning. They do not work in extreme cultural differences and in ethnic situations (63).
- E. Meyer, Chairman of Grey Advertising, is quoted as stating that high-tech products lend themselves more easily to globalisation, and also that products with a nationalistic flavour can take advantage of global marketing opportunities if the specific country has a good reputation in the field (20).
- World products, such as Universal Medical Products' disposable syringes, go for bigger markets; these are very high-volume goods made at low cost to a single design for everyone. They are insensitive to differences in their users (25).
- Consumer non-durables, low-tech assembly companies, heavy raw-material processing industries, wholesaling and service businesses are not suitable for global practices (64).
- Products that enjoy high economies of scale are not very culturally bound and are easier to market globally. Most packaged goods are less susceptible to economies of scale than durables. Younger people, frequent travellers and fashion followers generally use fewer culture-bound products (41).
- Food products, cleaning products, household appliances or other products related to home-centred roles are more likely to require adaptation to local markets. However, products purchased predominantly by minority segments (such as stereo components, health foods, cosmetics and herbal perfumes) do not require much adaptation. If the product is purchased by more sophisticated, innovative or affluent consumers, universal appeals fit more easily (50).
- An example from Deere Co. International is referred to. Although this company usually tested its brand's advertising in its agricultural *Furrow* magazine, it could not standardise its advertising in Latin America because different models were sold in each market (65).

4. *Market readiness*

- An example is given where a product from Acorn was positioned differently in different campaigns in the UK, USA and West Germany, according to the product's stage in its life-cycle (66).
- Apple is cited as an example that had to use local strategies because computer preparedness was different in each country (12).
- A look at the advertising business in eight Asian countries. The problems encountered were related to the country's economy and cultural characteristics (67).

Table 3.1 Continued.

- The problems faced in developing countries with regard to advertising are very different from those in developed countries. Illiteracy, hygiene, a lack of knowledge about birth control and a lack of nutrition should all be considered (68).

5. *Popular media in different countries*

- The Egyptians showed more interest in the media than the French. French attentiveness was lower in all media, except the cinema. Men spent more of their time involved in the media than women (69).
- Although the UK and France generally both emphasise the importance of cultural and intellectual life, the largest-selling newspapers are sensational types in both of these countries. This study asks whether or not the EEC is really such a mass market after all (37).
- A recommendation for the use of different media types when advertising with offensive (for young brands) and defensive (for mature brands) marketing strategies (70).
- A report on the differences in popular media types used by US and European agencies. European agencies prefer newspapers, magazines and outdoor more than US agencies (71).
- Specific examples given from eleven countries (72).
- An emphasis on the need to tailor media selection, even for different product groups (73).

6. *Differences in advertising messages*

- An exploration into the differences between American and Swedish advertising with the help of Clio winners and cinema commercials in terms of the advertising strategies used as well as how informative they are. Large differences are reported (74).
- A comparison of the information content of ads and their time of airing in Ecuador, the USA and Australia. The most informative ads were found in Ecuador, where there are more products in the introduction stages of their life-cycles (75).
- A measurement of advertising effectiveness on US citizens, Thais in the USA, foreigners in the USA and Thais in Thailand. It is argued that different advertisements are needed for foreigners living in the USA. Examples are given from McDonalds, Coca Cola and Kentucky Fried Chicken of advertising to blacks, Hispanics and to women (76).
- An analysis of press ads from the Philippines in terms of their advertising content within the framework of nine cultural parameters. The findings indicate that they do not reflect the indigenous culture of the Philippines but that of Western cultures. This also argues that the misuse of culture as a vehicle of communication should not be under-estimated (77).
- The different interpretations of advertising motifs caused by different perceptions across countries. The differently accepted norms and regulations (for example, in Spain, Denmark and Holland the wearing of the wedding ring on the right, not the left, hand) (78).
- How can the positioning of a car be standardised as 'sporty' where there is a 70-mph speed limit (79)?
- A comparative study of three product groups, examining US and Singaporean students' responses in their use of information sources. The findings indicate a lack of cultural differences in this respect, as both groups exhibited a heavy reliance on word-of-mouth advertising. This is one of the exceptions, where the findings do not show significant differences between two groups (80).
- Persuasive messages are easier to transfer from one culture to another. Whether the

Table 3.1 Continued.

source is native or foreign, the message attributed or not, or whether it was illustrated or not does not seem to make much difference. This study was conducted on urban French and Egyptians through print ads. It constitutes the second exception (81).

7. Advertising styles and types

- Referring to E. Meyer's views, this study mentions ads with visual appeal that avoid the problems of translation. Brands promoted with image campaigns also travel well, where themes with a universal appeal are used, such as eroticism and wealth (20).
- Japanese ads are full of emotion and entertainment rather than being based on an understanding of others through guessing; this is also reflected in the advertising (82).
- A suggestion to use emotional approaches when advertising to prospective buyers, but the use of rational arguments when advertising to near-to-actual buyers (83, 84).
- Retail advertising is emphasised as being more difficult to monitor by HQs. The retail-advertising technique requires local cultural knowledge (85).
- A report that sales-promotion agencies are finding it difficult to handle international promotions. Language differences, regulations and restrictions on the value of give-aways are cited as reasons for the problems faced (86).
- Although *Sky* magazine was launched as a pan-European magazine, different sales promotions and techniques are used in different countries to increase its sales (87).

could the same thing be achieved in international advertising? Or have agencies and companies already succeeded in creating localised but low-cost international advertising campaigns, having the same theme and look but a local style and tone? These questions are answered in Chapter 9, where it is shown how agency executives, as practitioners, cope with this dilemma in real-life situations.

THE WAY OUT: TOO MUCH TO HOPE FOR?

In practice, neither an entirely standardised nor an entirely localised advertising approach is used. If international advertising is seen as a continuum between totally centralised and totally decentralised local campaigns, then most brands will fall between the two extremes. A combination of the two approaches is generally put into use in varying ratios, as the market conditions and corporate objectives dictate.

Corporate executives are forced to take a broader view of this highly controversial area. After all, they carry the responsibility for their decisions. There are, reassuringly, some academics who also take the middle road on international advertising, and who do not insist on either extreme.

We shall first consider what the academics have to offer. Academics stress that flexibility is the key word in international advertising – they reject entirely considering global marketing/advertising as an either/or proposition. The essential question should be 'how to tailor the global marketing concept to fit each business and how to make it work' (41). The middle road that it is advised to follow is the one that blends, to some degree, uniformity with individual area differences. The whole idea of transferring international campaigns is based on looking at each case and country individually. There are no set and fixed rules that could be applied to every situation. For no matter what reason, global campaigns should not be forced upon any local market. If the campaign seems to be inappropriate in any way, the notion of transferring that campaign should be dropped at once.

The concept of 'pattern standardisation' emerges when discussing campaign transfers across countries. In pattern standardisation, the campaign – with its overall theme and individual elements – was originally designed to be used in multiple markets. In these campaigns there is a uniformity in direction but not necessarily in detail. The uniformity is in presentation, but the art-form is transliterated at the local level within specified variables. The campaign might end up not being used at all in its original form. Pattern standardisation requires the use of a single international agency that has a worldwide network. It is also accepted that MNCs will exert a certain degree of control over subsidiaries. Goodyear International is said to use pattern standardisation successfully in their international advertising activities (88).

Another practical recommendation is the creation of a centrally managed group to undertake the planning (26). This group should provide central management with objectives, as well as comply with them. The aim is to pool talents, making use of synergy for the product's benefit. Nonetheless, the execution of the resulting campaign pattern should be handled at the local level. It is also essential that the parties involved should be totally convinced of the improved outcome obtained by investing in corporate advertising. Only then can large sums of money be saved by the use of the cornorate-pattern concept.

Various lists exist that name the criteria to be fulfilled if international campaigns are to be transferred smoothly across borders. It is not feasible, however, to claim that they are exhaustive. These lists should, therefore, be regarded as rough measures to apply when trying to make decisions about the transfer of international campaigns. The most-mentioned measures are

- the homogeneity or heterogeneity of markets;
- the type of product (with or without a universal selling appeal);
- product positioning;
- foreign counterparts and the corporate organisation of the advertiser (whether or not it is truly multinational);
- maintaining home-office budget-approval authority;
- the cultural patterns in different markets;
- the economic and political climate in international markets;
- the extent to which consumerism is acknowledged;
- legal restrictions on the nature of advertising, trade codes, ethical practices and industry agreements;
- government tariffs on art-work or on printed matter;

- the characteristics, availability and acceptance of media;
- the services available to the advertising agency in each market (whether or not it has an international network);
- the qualifications of account executives in other international branches of the agency; and
- the detailed planning of lead times, especially in the activities of overseas markets (89, 90).

All the warnings given above are relevant and to the point, but the list is probably too short and not thorough enough: there are a great many other obstacles and stumbling blocks on the way to the smooth transfer of international campaigns across borders. In this book it is believed that we offer a more itemised list for the same purpose, with a big promise to practitioners – the 'Magic Checklist' given in Chapter 10 as the 'final say'! However, before going on to look at practitioners' working examples for running successful international campaigns, it is necessary to remember what Lowenthal (91) has said: 'Good ideas and good products must be timely to succeed!'

An example of the tools practitioners make use of when running successful international campaigns was given in Chapter 2 – the FCB Grid. Obviously there are many others. However, we wish here to include some less well-known and relatively more recent practices used in the advertising business. There is, for example, a definite general trend towards the use of pan-regional campaigns. In Europe, the use of pan-European advertising is becoming more and more popular: it is almost in fashion. Pan-regional brands are called the brands of the future, and the exploitation of similarities is advocated positively (9). It is even suggested that putting pan-European advertising into practice will lower marketing costs, which might easily account for 60–80% of product prices (92).

We now turn to a few examples of running international campaigns around the globe that were free of blunders, one of which is Coca Cola's football-star campaign, where different stars were used in different countries. While the theme was kept constant, the pattern was adapted to fit each country. It was reasoned that 'Global advertising is not "Take It. Translate It. Run It. Don't Argue!" Not even in Coca Cola!' (93). International advertising should succeed in tapping fundamental common feelings in different countries, without attempting to change the product's persona.

Another example comes from an international company that specialises in adapting communications. Ursula Grüber Communications Internationale SA is based in France, adapting rather than translating in 23 languages. The company has 200 freelance copywriters and journalists each living in their own countries. Each communicator translates only into his or her own language. Clients include companies as well as advertising agencies. The general belief is that the advertising message reflects the life-style, customs, mood and environment of the country where the product or service is being generated. It is therefore better to make use of the rich, native experience of locals (94, 95, 96).

Gillette is also reported as using regional advertising. This company has four, broad, geographical areas around the globe. Pan-group projects are developed by lead countries in these groups and then introduced into the other countries belonging to the same geographical area (12). The pan-European approach and the implementation of it adopted by Gillette was explained by account supervisor, Donna Delaine, at BBDO, London, during the author's interviews with agency executives. The Gillette way of handling international advertising is described in Chapter 7.

Finally and more recently, another pan-European advertisement produced by the French subsidiary of BBDO (CLM:BBDO) was reported in *The Financial Times*. This ad was developed for the International Wool Secretariat's 'Love from Woolmark' campaign. Other European BBDO subsidiaries had also collaborated in its creation. It was introduced into 16 European countries, using the same slogan, the copy being translated into 12 languages and appearing in pan-European media (97).

This is the current state of the debate on the issue of globalisation. The pros and cons have been explicitly stated throughout the chapter. The number of references given in this chapter is also evidence of how controversial international advertising can be. The studies undertaken point out that the successful standardisation of advertising is no easy task and, if practised, should be done with utmost care, caution and consideration. We will see how the international advertising agency executives who were interviewed cope with international advertising in Chapters 6–10. We will also show the ways they chose to take that eventually led them to successfully transferred global campaigns.

Chapter 4 deals with world advertising expenditure as well as with other figures to give the reader a hint of the advertising sector's dimensions. New trends and new developments taking place that will have an impact on the future of international advertising are also briefly mentioned. It may well be the time to march on with a different drummer . . .

REFERENCES

1. Buzzell, R. D. (1968) Can you standardize multinational marketing?, *Harvard Business Review*, November–December, pp. 102–13.
2. Keegan, W. J. (1970) Five strategies for multinational marketing, *European Business*, January, pp. 35–40.
3. Sands, S. (1979) Can you standardise international marketing strategy?, *Journal of the Academy of Marketing Science*, Vol. 7, no. 1 & 2, Winter/Spring, pp. 117–34.
4. Taking a long, hard look at where global marketing's going (1984) *Marketing and Media Decisions*, December, pp. 34–8, 40, 42, 108, 110, 112, 114, 116, 117, 126.
5. Earle, R. M. (1984) Global advertising, *Madison Avenue*, Vol. 26, no. 12, December, pp. 40–4.
6. Levitt, T. (1983) The globalization of markets, *Harvard Business Review*, May/June, pp. 92–102.
7. Draper, G. (1984) Go global or die, *Marketing*, Vol. 18, no. 6, 9 August, pp. 24–6.

8. Thomson, D. (1985) When is a global strategy advantageous?, *ADMAP*, September, pp. 423–30.
9. Winram, S. (1984) The opportunity for world brands, *International Journal of Advertising*, Vol. 3, no. 1, pp. 17–26.
10. McNally, G. J. (1986) It's not just possible – it's imperative, *Business Marketing*, April, pp. 64, 68, 70.
11. Thackray, J. (1985) Much ado about global marketing, *Across the Board*, Vol. 22, no. 4, April, pp. 38–46.
12. Rutigliano, A. J. (1986) The debate goes on: global versus local advertising, *Management Review*, Vol. 75, no. 6, June, pp. 27–31.
13. Ricks, D. A. and Mahajan, V. (1984) Blunders in international marketing, *Long Range Planning*, February, pp. 78–84.
14. Ricks, D. A. (1984) How to avoid business blunders abroad, *Business*, Vol. 34, no. 2, April–June, pp. 3–12.
15. Ricks, D. A., Arpan, J. S. and Fu, M. Y. (1974) Pitfalls in advertising overseas, *Journal of Advertising Research*, Vol. 14, no. 6, December, pp. 47–51.
16. Hawkins, S. (1983) How to understand your partner's cultural baggage, *International Management Europe*, September, pp. 48–51.
17. Almaney, A. (1974) Intercultural communication and the multinational company executive, *Columbia Journal of World Business*, Winter, pp. 23–8.
18. Lorenz, C. (1984) The overselling of world brands, *The Financial Times*, 19 July, p. 12.
19. Godfrey, L. (1985) The more global the approach the blander the message – must it be so?, *ADMAP*, September, pp. 428–30.
20. Fannin, R. (1984) What agencies really think of global theory, *Marketing and Media Decisions*, Vol. 19, no. 15, December, pp. 74–82.
21. Harris, G. (1984) The globalisation of advertising, *International Journal of Advertising*, Vol. 3, no. 3, pp. 223–35.
22. Harris, G. (1985) Global marketing and global agencies, *ADMAP*, Vol. 21, no. 9, September, pp. 420–2.
23. Sorenson, R. Z. and Wiechmann, U. E. (1975) How multinationals view marketing standardization, *Harvard Business Review*, Vol. 53, May–June, pp. 38–44, 48–50, 54, 166–7.
24. Terpstra, V. (1983) Critical mass and international marketing strategy, *Journal of the Academy of Marketing Science*, Vol. 11, no. 3, Summer, pp. 269–82.
25. Braidwood, S. (1984) World products, *Design*, September, no. 429, pp. 40–6.
26. Peebles, D. M. and Ryans, J. K. jr (1983) One international cultural philosophy, *International Advertiser*, January–February, Part II, pp. 16, 18.
27. International advertising grows (1979) in S. W. Dunn and E. S. Lorimor (eds.) *International Advertising and Marketing*, Grid Publications, Columbus, Ohio, pp. 79–86 (originally appeared in *The New World of Advertising*, Crain Books, Chicago. 1975).
28. Tamilia, R. D. (1979) International advertising revisited, in H. W. Berkman and I. R. Vernon (eds.) *Contemporary Perspectives in International Business*, Rand McNally, Chicago, Ill., pp. 197–205.
29. Marketing can be global, but ads must remain cultural (1987) *Marketing News*, 31 July, no. 7, pp. 26–8.
30. Boakes, N. (1989) The international dimension, in M. Thomas (ed.) *The Marketing Handbook*, Gower, Aldershot, pp. 113–21.
31. Bernstein, D. (1984) *Company Image and Reality*, Holt, Rinehart & Winston/The Advertising Association, Eastbourne.
32. Lodge, C. (1987) Getting to know foreign bodies, *Marketing*, 2 April, pp. 50–1.
33. Brassard, G. (1973) Translator is a must – ads have to speak the language, *Industrial Marketing*, Vol. 58, no. 12, December, pp. 76–8.

34. Hall, E. T. (1960) The silent language in overseas business, *Harvard Business Review*, Vol. 38, no. 3, May/June, pp. 87–96.
35. Code of Advertising Practice Committee (CAP) (1985) *The British Code of Advertising Practice*, London.
36. The Institute of Practitioners in Advertising (IPA) (1986) *About the IPA*, London, April.
37. Dunn, S. W. and Lorimor, E. S. (eds.) (1979) *International Advertising and Marketing*, Grid Publications, Columbus, Ohio.
38. Miracle, G. E. and Nevett, T. (1987) *Voluntary Regulation of Advertising*, Heath, Lexington, Mass.
39. Boddewyn, J. J. (1987) International advertisers face government hurdles, *Marketing News*, 8 May, pp. 20–1, 26.
40. Boddewyn, J. J. (1985) Global perspective on advertising control, in E. Kaynak (ed.) *Global Perspectives in Marketing*, Praeger Special Studies, New York, NY, pp. 37–51.
41. Quelch, J. A. and Hoff, E. J. (1986) Customizing global marketing, *Harvard Business Review*, Vol. 64, no. 3, May/June, pp. 59–69.
42. Going global (1986) *European Management Journal*, Spring, Vol. 4, no. 1, pp. 10–28.
43. Ogilvy, D. (1983) *Ogilvy on Advertising*, Pan Books, London.
44. Brooke, M. Z. (1986) *International Management*, Hutchinson, London.
45. Dunn, S. W. and Yorke D. A. (1974) European executives look at advertising, *Columbia Journal of World Business*, Vol. 9, Winter, pp. 54–60.
46. Christian, D. (1974) European views of advertising, *Journal of Advertising*, Vol. 3, no. 4, Fall, pp. 23–5.
47. Anderson, R. D., Engledow, J. L. and Becker, H. (1978) Advertising attitudes in West Germany and the US: an analysis over age and time, *Journal of International Business Studies*, Vol. IX, no. 3, Winter, pp. 27–38.
48. Wills, J. R. jr and Ryans, J. K. jr (1982) Attitudes toward advertising: a multinational study, *Journal of International Business Studies*, Vol. 13, no. 3, Winter, pp. 121–9.
49. Caffyn, J. and Rogers, N. (1970) British reactions to TV commercials, *Journal of Advertising Research*, Vol. 10, no. 3, June, pp. 21–7.
50. Douglas, S. P. and Urban, C. D. (1977) Life style analysis to profile women in international markets, *Journal of Marketing*, Vol. 41, July, pp. 46–54.
51. Urban, C. D. (1975) Life style analysis, *Marketing News*, 5 December, p. 11.
52. Green, R. T., Cunningham, W. and Cunningham, I. C. M. (1975) The effectiveness of standardized advertising, *Journal of Advertising*, Vol. 4, Summer, pp. 25–9.
53. Green, R. T. and Cunningham, I. C. M. (1980) Family purchasing roles in two countries, *Journal of International Business Studies*, Vol. XI, no. 1, Spring/Summer, pp. 92–7.
54. Etzel M. J. and Walker, B. J. (1974) Advertising strategy for foreign products, *Journal of Advertising Research*, Vol. 14, no. 3, June, pp. 41–4.
55. Martenson, R. (1987) Is standardisation of marketing feasible in culture-bound industries? A European case study, *International Marketing Review*, Autumn, pp. 7–17.
56. Plummer, J. T. (1977) Consumer focus in cross national research, *Journal of Advertising*, Spring, pp. 5–15.
57. Dunn, S. W. (1966) The case study approach in cross-cultural research, *Journal of Marketing Research*, Vol. 3, February, pp. 26–31.
58. Ryans, J. K. jr (1969) Is it too soon to put a tiger in every tank?, *Columbia Journal of World Business*, Vol. IV, March/April, pp. 69–75.
59. Suzuki, N. (1980) The changing pattern of advertising strategy by Japanese business firms in the US market: content analysis, *Journal of International Business Studies*,

Vol. XI, no. 3, Winter, pp. 63–72.
60. Pitcher, A. E. (1985) The role of branding in international advertising, *International Journal of Advertising*, Vol. 4, pp. 241–6.
61. Lorimor, E. S. (1979) A look at some current articles in international advertising and marketing, in S. W. Dunn and E. S. Lorimor (eds.) *International Advertising and Marketing*, Grid Publications, Columbus, Ohio, pp. 55–66.
62. Ritchie, R. (1986) Global branding need not mean global advertising, *ADMAP*, January, pp. 39–42.
63. Diaz, R. M. (1985) Advertising in foreign markets, *SAM Advanced Management Journal*, Vol. 50, no. 4, Autumn, pp. 12–20.
64. Hout, T., Porter, M. E. and Rudden, E. (1982) How global companies win out, *Harvard Business Review*, September/October, pp. 98–108.
65. Paskowski, M. (1981) Deere and Co. — international marketing foundation for successful future growth, *Industrial Marketing*, Vol. 66, no. 2, February, pp. 66–70.
66. McEwan, F. (1984) A dichotomy in campaign style, *The Financial Times*, 26 January (Management Page), p. 14.
67. Weinstein, A. K. (1970) Development of an advertising industry in Asia, *MSU Business Topics*, Spring, pp. 28–36.
68. Tal, E. (1974) Advertising in developing countries, *Journal of Advertising*, Vol. 3, no. 2, Spring, pp. 19–23.
69. Lorimor, E. S. and Dunn, S. W. (1968–9) Use of the mass media in France and Egypt, *Public Opinion Quarterly*, Vol. 32, Winter, pp. 680–7.
70. Bruno, A. V., Hustad, T. P. and Pessemier, E. A. (1980). Media approaches to segmentation, in D. W. Scotton and R. L. Zallocco (eds.) *Readings in Market Segmentation*, AMA, Chicago, Ill., pp. 143–50.
71. McGann, A. F. and Aaby, N. E. (1975) The advertising industry in Western Europe, *Journal of Advertising*, Vol. 4, no. 3, Summer, pp. 19–24, 35.
72. How Colgate uses media in 11 diverse countries (1979) in S. W. Dunn and E. S. Lorimor (eds.) *International Advertising and Marketing*, Grid Publications, Columbus, Ohio, pp. 157–70 (originally published in *International Marketing and Media*, Vol. 10, no. 1, January, 1975, pp. 96–102).
73. Summers, A. (1986) Sustaining a multiproduct brand name, *ADMAP*, January, pp. 29–38.
74. Martenson, R. (1987) Content in American and Swedish advertising, *International Journal of Advertising*, Vol. 6, pp. 133–44.
75. Renforth, W. and Raveed, S. (1983) Consumer information cues in TV advertising: a cross-country analysis, *Journal of the Academy of Marketing Science*, Vol. 11, no. 3, Summer, pp. 216–25.
76. Onkvisit, S. and Shaw, J. J. (1983–4) Identifying marketing attributes necessary for standardised international advertising, *Mid-Atlantic Journal of Business*, Vol. 22, no. 1, Winter, pp. 43–57.
77. Marquez, F. T. (1975) The relationship of advertising and culture in the Philippines, *Journalism Quarterly*, Vol. 52, no. 3, Autumn, pp. 436–42.
78. Dunn, S. W. and Barban, A. W. (1986) *Advertising: Its Role in Modern Marketing* (6th edn), CBS College Publishing, New York, NY.
79. Gratia, M. J. (1984) The European advertising of the Ford Sierra: a comparative study in Belgium, the UK and Luxembourg (BSc dissertation), UMIST, Manchester.
80. Tan, C. T. and Dolich, I. J. (1983) A comparative study of consumer information seeking: Singapore versus US, *Journal of the Academy of Marketing Science*, Vol. 11, no. 3, Summer, pp. 313–22.
81. Lorimor, E. S. and Dunn, S. W. (1968) Reference groups, congruity theory and

cross-cultural persuasion, *The Journal of Communication*, Vol. 18, December, pp. 354–68.
82. Ishikawa, M. (1987) Latest trends in Japanese advertising (paper presented at the Fifteenth World Industrial Advertising Congress), Brussels.
83. Einar, L. (1987) Working with advertising agencies (paper presented at the Fifteenth World Industrial Advertising Congress), Brussels.
84. Berger, D. (1986) Theory into practice: the FCB Grid, *European Research*, Vol. 14, no. 1, pp. 35–46.
85. Peebles, D. M. and Ryans, J. K. jr (1984) *Management of International Advertising – A Marketing Approach*, Allyn & Bacon, Boston, Mass.
86. Hall, D. (1987) Learning the global language, *Marketing*, 19 February, pp. 40–1.
87. An international move for media (1987) *Marketing*, 2 April, pp. 46–9.
88. Peebles, D. M., Ryans, J. K. jr and Vernon, I. R. (1977) A new perspective on advertising standardisation, *European Journal of Marketing*, Vol. 11, pp. 569–76.
89. Miracle, G. E. (1968) International advertising principles and strategies, *MSU Business Topics*, Vol. 16, Fall, pp. 29–36.
90. Dunn, S. W. (1976) Effect of national identity on multinational promotional strategy in Europe, *Journal of Marketing*, Vol. 40, no. 4, October, pp. 50–7.
91. Lowenthal, A. D. (1978) Too soon or too late, good ideas, products can fail here, overseas, *Marketing News*, Vol. 11, no. 18, 10 March, p. 3.
92. Elinder, E. (1965) How international can European advertising be?, *Journal of Marketing*, Vol. 29, April, pp. 7–11.
93. Day, B. (1985) Global advertising: the facts and the fantasy, *ADMAP*, September, pp. 434–7.
94. The tricky world of language (1985) *International Advertiser*, Vol. 12, no. 5, October, pp. 7–8.
95. The creative business of language adaptation (1982) *International Advertiser*, March/April, p. 20.
96. Some do's and don'ts for advertising successfully beyond the language barrier (Company report, courtesy of Ursula Grüber Communications Internationale SA).
97. Rawsthorn, A. (1989) Turning people on to wool, *The Financial Times*, 26 January.

4

MARCHING ON WITH A DIFFERENT DRUMMER: WHAT THE FUTURE HOLDS

THE LION'S SHARE IN WORLD ADVERTISING EXPENDITURE

The Advertising Association, in their annual commentary, note that 1987 was a year when advertising expenditure in the UK in both absolute and relative terms climbed to record levels. UK advertising expenditure reached £5,781 million, accounting for 1.38% of gross national product (GNP) at market prices, and 2.22% of consumer expenditures. Total expenditure adds up to £6,264 million when direct mail is included (1). In 1988, in the UK, total expenditure reached £6,779 million, with an increase rate of 17% over 1987 advertising expenditure. Annual advertising expenditures in 1988 constituted 1.46% of GNP at market prices, and 2.33% of consumer expenditures. Total expenditure including direct mail reached £7,309 million in 1988. Table 4.1 shows each medium's share in the total UK advertising expenditure for the years 1987 and 1988.

Table 4.1 Different media's share of the UK's 1987 and 1988 total advertising expenditure

Medium	1987 expenditure		1988 expenditure	
	(£m)	(%)	(£m)	(%)
Press	3,560	61.6	4,242	62.5
TV	1,872	32.4	2,127	31.4
Poster and transportation	0.216	3.7	0.244	3.6
Radio	0.111	1.9	0.139	2.1
Cinema	0.022	0.4	0.027	0.4
Total	5,781	100.0	6,779	100.0

(*Source*: Reference 1.)

As for Europe, it is reported that, in 1985, total expenditure amounted to 29,566 million European Currency Unit (ECU). The same expenditure figure jumped to 32,942 million ECU in 1986, yielding an annual increase of 11% (1). The increase rate of the UK's advertising expenditure in 1986 was 15%. The same expenditure figure was 13% in 1987. These values demonstrate the steadier growth rates in the UK compared to the whole of Europe. In 1988, Europe's advertising expenditure reached 36,442 million ECU, with an increase rate of 11%.

The Starch Inra Survey (2) reveals a 20% increase in world advertising expenditure in 1987 over 1986. Total world figures for 1987 and 1988, as well as the four highest spender countries, are included in Table 4.2. Compared to 1987, world advertising expenditure in 1988 exhibited a slower growth rate, with a 10% increase rate as against the 20% of the previous year. Japan still continued to show the highest growth rate of the four. The UK's and West Germany's advertising expenditures are close to each other in amount as well as in rates of growth. In Table 4.2, the USA emerges as the world advertising-expenditure leader. The rate of increase in Japan, as well as in the UK and West Germany, is far ahead of Europe – and the world total, for that matter. The USA currently accounts for just over half the total world expenditure. However, this trend is expected to alter: the deregulation of television, the introduction of the Single Market in 1992 and the high advertising growth rates of the Iberian Peninsula, the southern Mediterranean, Latin America and Asia–Pacific countries all imply that the demand for marketing services from markets outside the USA will become even greater in the near future (3).

What's more, figures given in Tables 4.1 and 4.2 help to highlight the significance of this particular study narrated in the book for the advertising world: no matter which table you look at or which currency you adopt, the UK is the world's third largest spender country in advertising. The results obtained, therefore, and reported here, are valid for the third largest advertising spender country in the world.

Table 4.2 World advertising expenditures (1987 and 1988) and the highest four spender countries

	1987 ($m)	1988 ($m)	(% increase)
World total	206,440.6	228,000.0	+10
USA	109,650.0	118,050.0	+8
Japan	27,273.2	34,471.3	+26
UK	10,266.0	12,076.0	+18*
West Germany	9,985.8	11,750.1	+18

Note
* The different increase rates given for UK expenditure are because of the use of different currencies in the calculations.

(*Source*: Reference 2.)

THE GROWING IMPORTANCE OF ADVERTISING

The 1980s are generally acknowledged as the period when third-wave agencies blossomed, mainly led by the growth of Saatchi & Saatchi (S & S), WPP and other publicly quoted agencies. The use of advertising by political parties also became common practice in the UK. The Conservatives' third victory was credited to the S & S brothers' efforts.

After 1986, Her Majesty's Government surfaced as the UK's largest single advertiser, mostly as a result of advertising for different campaigns. This was after political parties had started to use advertising actively for their own propaganda purposes: government expenditure in advertising was a mere £31 million in 1979; in 1986 the same expenditure figure left peer groups in open-mouthed amazement, reaching £81.4 million (4). The chief impetus behind this high government-advertising spending in the late 1980s was the privatisation of various British enterprises. Following the privatisation of British Telecom, the flotation of British Gas and British Petrol all contributed to this high advertising-expenditure level.

The 1980s also saw the advertising world playing a major role in tackling sensitive social issues (5). These were mainly involved with the AIDS and anti-heroin campaigns developed by TBWA early in 1987. They were followed by the Youth Training campaign 'Action for Jobs', the 'Keep Your Country Tidy', the 'Let's Crack Crime' campaigns, and the like, run in 1988. As the ethics of advertising is a long-debated issue (6), this had a special significance in improving advertising agencies' long-standing poor image in the eyes of the public. Agencies proved they can handle social issues, and undertake social responsibility without any intention of selling a product or service.

Another recent development that emphasises the role of advertising in society is environmentalism. As consumers are growing more and more environmentally conscious, corporates need to be in a position to say to their consumers: 'Buy our products and be part of the solution'. In order to be able to deliver this message, companies desperately need advertising's help. Advertising's role as an important and efficient source of information about a brand is shown strikingly in the following anecdote. Procter & Gamble's (P & G) environmental chief, Geoff Place, in a visit to his brother's family in the UK, found out that the family no longer used P & G products because of environmental concerns. Later he was informed that they had switched back to P & G products after they had become aware of a new statement on labels: P & G had since included 'Only biodegradable surface active agents used in this product'. The odd thing was that that had been the case since 1963 (7). The moral is, whatever the corporate's claim may be, be it less packaging to throw away, recycled or recyclable products or packaging material, or avoiding CFCs, they should be able to communicate this to their consumers. Corporates could be avid followers of green-marketing but if they do not transmit this message, they will not benefit from their responsible actions, as in the P & G case. This is, therefore, another area where advertising will continue to play a major and crucial role throughout the 1990s.

Apart from the traditionally known big spenders in advertising, such as the USA and other Western countries, other countries also started to show expansion in advertising in the 1980s. These countries, for example, Saudi Arabia, Jordan, Oman, South Africa and Greece, exhibited 100% or more increase rates in their advertising expenditures in 1987 (2). Furthermore, no one could deny the changes that took place in China (8), the Soviet Union and East European countries (9) during the 1980s, especially at the end of the decade and in 1990. The effects on their advertising brought about by opening up to Western influences were also reflected in the changes taking place in their political climate. To keep pace with these developments, Ford, Pepsi Cola and Sony advertisements were shown on Soviet television in May 1988 just before President Reagan's visit to Moscow for the May 1988 Summit. Hungary's first commercial TV channel, Mtv Plusz, was launched in May 1988. The initial plan was to buy foreign films, international sports events and language programmes with the money made from advertising.

International agencies seem to be competing with each other in trying to set up partnerships in East European countries. DMB & B is concentrating efforts to establish its Russian branch without any further delay. Young & Rubicam (Y & R) and O & M are trying to secure their positions in former Eastern Bloc countries through their existing offices in Moscow and Budapest (which were established in 1989). McCann-Erickson Worldwide and S & S are doing likewise. Y & R/Sovero already has 13 clients in the USSR, with expected profits of $1.5 million for 1990. O & M is hopeful that their annual billings will increase at a rate of 20% with their Hungarian partner, Mahir (10). East European countries are definitely considered as vast, untouched and promising markets in the areas of marketing and communications. Between December 1989 and March 1990 it is reported that 64 Western media giants made attempts to enter the Hungarian private-television and press business. The French businessman, Hersant, is already in the Russian market with the magazine, *Businessman*, in Russian, and *Business in the USSR* in English. Romania has had its *Free Youth* magazine since early 1990 (11).

All in all, advertising is expanding all around the globe without any differentiation for different political systems. A worldwide annual increase rate of 10–20% is a high percentage to be ignored by any industry and for any reason. As the number of countries eagerly engaged in advertising increases, the importance of international advertising naturally grows. This trend is, by itself, strong enough to force both agencies and advertisers to make international advertising work across borders.

THE NEW MEDIA – CABLE AND SATELLITE CHANNELS

In Europe, cable and satellite channels are expected to expand the role of television advertising. European countries, only a few years away from 1992, still exhibit major discrepancies in their advertising regulations, from copyright infringement and cultural restrictions to the prohibition of advertising in broadcast media. One can even cite restrictions on commercial airing times and durations (12, 13). As the new media emerge, governments are faced with another dilemma: whether or not to apply the same standards to advertising in their countries (maintaining a uniform code of practice) or to relax advertising restrictions. If they stick to a uniform code of practice, that will restrict growth. It will invest most of the power in the hands of current broadcasters. On the other hand, if advertising restrictions are relaxed, then programmes may become more entertainment orientated. In the latter case, traditional broadcasters will compete with each other (13). It is believed that, as pan-European services evolve, advertising revenues will be redistributed in the countries. Revenues will pour into the countries that originate transmissions instead of into those that view the programmes. This turn of events has raised serious concern for British programme makers. For instance, TVS Entertainment's full-page ad appeared in *The Sunday Times* (14) with the headline, 'Italian housewives do it on TV', stressing that – as satellite stations start operating in the UK in 1989 – the demand for new programmes will rise. As the competition becomes fierce among programme makers, they will seek ways of cutting down their costs in order to stay in the market. Cutting costs will most probably lead to compromises on high-quality material. The TVS Entertainment ad warns of a likely fall in programme quality.

Satellite and cable channels are, therefore, not free from problems regarding the screening of advertising, and most of these problems are still far from being solved. Nevertheless, agencies and advertisers believe in satellite and cable and promote them positively. For instance, S & S's Joint Deputy Managing Director is quoted as saying: 'The effect of satellite will be so profound that companies will start looking at Europe and divide it not along religious and economic lines, but according to satellite footprints' (15, p. 25). The support given by agencies and advertisers is crucial for the new media, otherwise it will not have a chance of survival without advertising's financial back-up. At the beginning of the 1990s, the state of UK satellite broadcasting seems rather gloomy. It is said that Sky Channel's weekly loss amounts to $3.5 million. The number of UK households receiving it is about 1.1 million. Super Channel fares no better: it is received in 14 European countries and enters 20 million households, but it is also losing money. Commentators agree that the major hurdle satellite broadcasting needs to overcome is language. It is no easy task to communicate to the 325 million consumers of Europe and be effective at the same time. However, all these problems are part of the learning curve: no doubt they will be solved and solved forever, because satellite broadcasting is already part of the lives of Europeans.

DISHARMONY IN EUROPE: TOWARDS 1992?

Another new wave is sweeping through Europe that also calls for drastic changes in the advertising strategies of international advertisers: the efforts to establish a single market by 1992 (16). Although much has been said and written about 1992, there is still much confusion among advertisers and agencies. Agencies are in a sort of strange rush to try to prove to their clients how they can serve them better in the single market. Full-page ads appear, listing why agencies are in a stronger position to give services under these new circumstances (17).

As has already been said, advertising regulations and legislation are far from uniform among member states. Rijkens and Miracle (18) review the allegations raised against advertising by consumerist organisations since the late 1960s, listing the events in chronological order. They point out that 'The saga of European regulation of advertising will continue. Commissioners will come and go. One consumer programme will replace another. Directives will be proposed, amended, withdrawn or approved' (*ibid.* p. 246). Without going into too much detail, it is necessary to report on the latest stage the Council of Europe, Committee of Ministers' draft directive has reached on the issue of the 'European Convention on Transfrontier Television' at their extraordinary meeting of 15 March 1989 in Strasbourg. Although this directive was not signed in May 1989, it was open for signature by member states (19). In this, advertising is covered in Chapter III, articles 11–16.

The draft directive states openly that neither subliminal nor surreptitious advertising will be allowed, especially when the presentation of products serves advertising purposes in programmes (article 13). The amount of advertising will not exceed 15% of daily transmission time (article 12). Feature films and films made for television (excluding series, serials, light entertainment and documentaries) that are longer than 45 minutes can be interrupted once for each complete period of 45 minutes. News and current-affairs programmes, documentaries, religious programmes and children's programmes that are shorter than 30 minutes will not be interrupted by advertisements (article 14). Tobacco advertisements are banned, but alcoholic beverage advertisements are permitted within certain limitations. For example, undue emphasis should not be placed on alcoholic content, and ads should not link the consumption of alcohol with performance or social or sexual success. Medicines that are only available on prescription will not be advertised (article 15). These, then, are the major guidelines that were adopted most recently, mainly covering basic regulatory points for harmonising European advertising legislation.

Although the Council of Ministers agreed on this directive in April 1989, several member states had certain reservations about it during the second reading in the European Parliament. These differences were finally ironed out, and the Broadcasting Directive was adopted on 3 October 1989. It was agreed that member states will implement the directive by 3 October 1991. The directive achieves three single-market goals (20, 21):

- Removing obstacles to the freedom of movement of services. This will enable member states to accept each other's transfrontier broadcasting. Only the retransmission of broadcasts that infringe the rules can be suspended.

- Protecting consumers by maintaining certain standards in programmes (the protection of minors against exposure to pornography or gratuitous violence).
- Providing an agreed regime on the amount, frequency and ethics of advertising, thus facilitating free trade in broadcasting services.

The points mentioned with regard to the draft directive were adopted in the council directive in Chapter IV, articles 10–21. It is also stated explicitly that television advertising should not prejudice respect for human dignity or include any discrimination on the grounds of race, sex or nationality, or be offensive to religious or political beliefs, or encourage behaviour against health, safety or the protection of the environment.

All these signs indicate that international advertising will flourish in the coming years. Agencies and advertisers, therefore, should be fully equipped to meet the demands set by global advertising practices. These developments are another big chunk in the gigantic jigsaw puzzle of international advertising. We wish to emphasise here that these are just a few of the issues that affect the successful transfer of international campaigns – the main theme of this book. No doubt these events will have an impact, but this book is not about the 'new media' or the 'single market' (and hence we did not go into too much detail about these). Instead, we hope to relate them to international clients, their agencies and to their campaigns. Having given some thought to the latest advances in international advertising, we can look at the role of HQs in advertising: how far do HQs become involved and how far should they? Is it possible to draw a line? If so, how is it drawn? Who should draw it? In short, it is now time to turn to power philosophies.

The advertising industry worldwide experienced a major hickup in 1990 and early 1991. For instance, in the USA the 1990 growth rate was 3.8% versus 8% in 1988. A similar trend is expected in the USA in 1991, between 3–4% growth rate (22). The UK agencies experienced the same ill-effects with a forecast 3.1% annual growth rate until 1992 against a 17% growth rate in 1988 (23). Note that these latest growth rates are well below the inflation rates of these countries. Many job losses in the USA and in the UK are also reported (23, 24). A sound general view of the advertising industry is given in *The Advertising Industry Survey* (25). In addition, more on 1992 with implications for the US firms is now available in other secondary sources (26, 27, 28).

REFERENCES

1. The Advertising Association (1988–9) *Advertising Statistical Yearbook*, sixth annual edition, London.
2. Starch Inra Hooper Inc. in co-operation with the International Advertising Association (1988–9) *Twenty-Second and Twenty-Third Survey of World Advertising Expenditures*, New York, NY.
3. What does WPP stand for? (1988) *The Sunday Times*, 19 June, p. D5.

4. Churchill, D. (1987) Government is big spender, *The Financial Times Survey*, section III, 29 October, p. II.
5. *Britain's advertising industry 1988* (1989) Jordan & Sons, Bristol.
6. Ferrell, O. C. (1985) Implementing and monitoring ethics in advertising, in G. R. Laczniak and P. E. Murphy (eds.) *Marketing Ethics*, Heath, Lexington, Mass., pp. 27–40.
7. Kirkpatrick, D. (1990) Environmentalism: the new crusade, *Fortune*, 12 February, pp. 44–52.
8. Russell, T. and Verrill, G. (1986) *Otto Klepner's Advertising Procedure* (9th edn), Prentice-Hall, Englewood Cliffs, NJ.
9. United Nations Committee report on the development of trade (1985) Sixth Seminar on East–West Trade Promotion, Marketing and business contacts, Geneva, 25–7 March.
10. Dogu bloku'nu reklam ajanslari parselliyor (1990) *Ekonomik Bulten*, 19–25 March, p. 11 (in Turkish).
11. Medya yatirimcilari dogu cikarmasinda (1990) *Gunes*, 31 March, p. 9 (in Turkish).
12. Paskowski, M. (1984) US programmers face off for global challenge, *Marketing and Media Decisions*, December, pp. 56–60, 126, 128, 130.
13. Tydeman, J. and Jakes Kelm, E. (1986) *New Media in Europe*, McGraw-Hill, Maidenhead.
14. Italian housewives do it on TV (1988) *The Sunday Times*, 18 September, p. A19.
15. Jivani, A. (1985) Where global obstacles lie, *Marketing*, 4 July, pp. 20–6.
16. The Department of Trade and Industry (1988) *The Single Market: Europe Open for Business*, London, September.
17. How do you feel about going into Europe? (1988) *The Financial Times*, 29 June, p. 5.
18. Rijkens, R. and Miracle, G. E. (1986) *European Regulation of Advertising*, Elsevier Science Publishers, North-Holland.
19. Council of Europe, Committee of Ministers' Draft Directive (1989) European Convention on Transfrontier Television (extraordinary meeting of the Committee of Ministers), Strasbourg, 22 March.
20. 'European vision for film and TV' and 'Broadcasting Directive' (1989) *Single Market News*, DTI, Issue No. 5, Winter, pp. 1, 4.
21. *Council Directive on Pursuit of Television Broadcasting Activities* (1989), The Council of the European Communities, Luxembourg, 3 October.
22. Coen, R.J. (1991) Coen: Little ad growth, *Advertising Age*, 20 May, pp. 1, 3.
23. Wentz, L. (1990) UK shops face hard times, *Advertising Age*, 6 August, p. 6.
24. Winski, J.M. (1990) Unemployed, *Advertising Age*, 12 November, pp. 28, 29, 31.
25. Micklethwait, J. (1990) The advertising industry, *The Economist*, 6 June, pp. 1–18.
26. Catoline, J. (1990) The European market in 1992: strategies for U.S. companies, *SAM Advances Management Journal*, Spring, pp. 33–41.
27. Harrison, G.J. (1988), The European Community's 1992 plan: an overview of the proposed 'Single Market', CRS Report Congress, Congressional Research Service, The Library of Congress, 21 September.
28. Calingaert, M. (1988), *The 1992 challenge from Europe: development of the European Community's internal market*, National Planning Association, Washington, D.C.

5
THE URGE TO POWER: HQ'S ROLE IN ADVERTISING

OUT-MANOEUVRING INTERNATIONAL MARKETING

Multinational corporations (MNCs) are, of course, faced with more uncontrollable market elements than domestic companies that limit their trade to their native markets. However, in spite of the problems they are faced with, more and more companies choose to go abroad and, as a result, they have to learn how to survive in world markets. It is a fact that, today, 50% of all economic activity in the world is international (1). It is expected that this trend will continue at an ever-increasing rate in the coming years.

At the beginning of the 1980s, corporates were grouped into two categories: the globetrotters and the globewatchers. For the globewatchers, prospects were not very bright. The forecasts were that they would face more and more competition from overseas firms in their own home markets. For the globetrotters, the important question was how to adapt their marketing strategy to existing market conditions (2). Success in international marketing lies in the art of bringing international strategy into harmony with the surrounding market structure. In international marketing, the market structure, the local marketing environment and the internation interface should be studied very seriously. International firms, therefore, need to be detail-orientated in order to gain a global competitive advantage. Alternatively, more and more companies find themselves pushed into the arena of international marketing to preserve their competitiveness. Once in the arena, the question arises of how to fight. To have a good start, firms need to be first movers: it is crucial to act (instead of reacting) to the changing dynamics of competition (1). In other words, MNCs should try to be the trend-setters, not the followers. Such an attitude could actually give them a competitive edge in international markets.

It is predicted that, in the 1990s, there will be an integration within world regions, not in the world as a whole. It is anticipated that, in the main, three forces will affect international marketing: a continuing integration of the world economy, technological change and a more globalised competitive environment (3). For the product, the internationalisation of product development, a shortening of product life-cycles, the globalisation of products and collaborative efforts in product development are foreseen. In promotions, a gradual and steady increase in the globalisation of the advertising message is expected. This will result from the continuing integration and growth of international advertising agencies and the growth of international market segments. Together with the globalisation of the advertising message, an internationalisation of advertising media is also predicted.

In general, therefore, international marketing seems to have moved away from globalisation towards a regional approach. Only Terpstra (3) does not mention regiocentric strategy, but continues to use globalisation. Furthermore, international advertising is perceived as an extension of international marketing. As a result, international advertising is expected to take corporates into the next century. Globalisation (or regionalisation) is said to be the watchword for foreign marketing in the coming decades. Additionally, the examples given for a pan-regional or, more specifically, for a pan-European approach in international advertising look more realistic and sound more convincing than the 'literal' meaning of 'global advertising'. That is why, as long as there is international marketing and advertising, we will continue to see HQ involvement alongside them. As there is no hope of getting rid of international marketing in the foreseeable future, we had better learn how to live with HQ involvement peacefully. The next section, therefore, is dedicated to subsidiaries, who do not view HQ involvement very favourably. They will be relieved to see they are not alone – there are others in the same boat and who share the same views.

POWER PHILOSOPHIES

HQs' role in subsidiary activities is a myth – and myths die hard. Subsidiaries usually consider their HQs as an 'overhead'. In a recent article, the way HQs are perceived is summed up as 'guilty until proven innocent' (4). Four types of HQ are identified (5):

- *Targeting*, which define fundamental objectives and set targets, but delegate operating decisions.
- *Guiding*, which co-ordinate business strategies, providing inputs to major operating decisions.
- *Directing*, which participate in the development of business strategies and in major operating decisions.
- *Running*, which develop and monitor plans, policies, guidelines and take major operating decisions.

HQs can adopt a more decentralised approach if there is (6):

- uncertainty and high risk in doing business abroad;
- heterogeneity in the foreign environment;

- a diversity of product line; and
- if subsidiaries account for a higher percentage in the total corporate sales.

On the other hand, HQs take the leading role in determining the

- strategic mission for the local operation;
- timing of new launches;
- targeted level of market shares;
- appropriate level of investment; and
- appropriate level of expected cash flow (7).

What's more, the role undertaken by the centre changes from one management function to another. The HQ's role is said to be 'active' in strategic planning, while altering to be 'reactive' in financial control (8). When it comes to HQ involvement in marketing activities, this is said to lead to multimarketing synergy (9). If the HQ acts as a co-ordinating body, then the market intelligence gained in one market can be applied to another comparable market. This means a better use of manpower and cost savings: the marketing programme is not duplicated in each country. The effectiveness of different programmes can be tested in different markets. In the end, the corporate can find a better programme as a result of experimentation. All this sounds very logical, sensible and plain, but we will see whether or not it is easier said than done: we shall look at what boosts and what eases HQ involvement in subsidiaries.

BALANCING THE POWER

Many factors affect the extent of HQ involvement in subsidiary activities. To begin with, the size of the HQ itself has a relation to the degree of involvement exercised over subsidiaries: as HQs become bigger, they become more involved. For example, targeting HQs have a personnel of 20 to 100, whereas directing headquarters have up to 13,000 (5). It is also argued that smaller international operations cannot afford to have a highly specialised multi-level staff, who hence end up having less control over their subsidiaries (10). As to the size of the subsidiary, smaller foreign operations are generally subject to more centralisation (11). This can be explained with the help of an example from Roussel Uclaf. It is claimed that their English subsidiary enjoys more autonomy than its Peruvian or Venezuelan counterparts, as the 'English subsidiary is older, bigger, far more vertically integrated and less dependent on the parent company' (6).

There are conflicting views on the degree of HQ involvement in the initial stages of subsidiary development. Some maintain that subsidiaries rely more on their parent companies when they are becoming established (12); however, others specify that subsidiaries are more autonomous in their early stages of investment, mainly because the initial investment is small and HQs confess to being unfamiliar with local environments (13).

Subsidiary performance is another factor that affects the control exercised by HQs: if subsidiaries fail to meet their targets they experience more intervention from their HQs. Consequently, successful subsidiaries are more loosely controlled than operations that are in severe difficulties (10, 14, 15). In Henkel, states von Briskorn, strong national brands are not standardised (16), although Aydin and Terpstra (17) point out that HQs make more recommendations for improving the performance of their Turkish subsidiaries if targets are not met. Aydin and Terpstra also suggest another possibility: the parent company becomes more involved if subsidiary sales account for higher percentages in the total parent-company sales. In short, whether subsidiaries exhibit a good or bad performance they cannot win – either way, both well-established and less-established subsidiaries experience HQ involvement, only for different reasons and with a different tone from their HQs.

Extensive communications between HQs and subsidiaries can lead to subsidiary marketing activities that are more standardised (18); similarly, when subsidiaries provide more detailed reporting, this can invite a high degree of HQ direction (13). The extent of HQ involvement also depends upon the business environment and the climate: if there are substantial environmental differences between the HQ and its subsidiary countries, then more responsibilities are delegated to local management. A plan to measure performance will not be relevant in a country where instability is high. Under these conditions, on-the-spot decisions are needed, which forces decision-making to be delegated to local managers (10). However, a further study has reported conflicting views: US parents intervene more in Mexican subsidiaries if HQs perceive discrepancies between the two countries' cultures (19). Obviously, the specific subsidiary countries studied must affect the results and, furthermore, even the same MNCs can (and do) alter their approach towards standardisation over time and according to the conditions under which they operate. For example, during World War II, Nestlé's local European managers enjoyed more autonomy to enable the expansion of Nestlé, to minimise disruptions in distribution and to respond to consumer needs. However, Vevey now practises tighter marketing control over its affiliated companies (14).

Overall, these and many other factors have an impact on the final outcome of HQ involvement in subsidiary activities – and this is why it is so difficult to predict the degree of HQ involvement. The size of HQs change, subsidiaries expand or shrink, they have ups and downs in performance, the business environment varies from one location to another, or extraordinary circumstances demand extraordinary measures, such as the war years. Taking all these intricate factors into account, one is not astonished at the delicacy of this balance; instead, one understands why the balance of power is so difficult to achieve and, if achieved, why it is so difficult to maintain it afterwards.

CONTROLLING 'HQ CONTROL' IN MARKETING

Standardisation should not be the general rule in marketing in subsidiary countries: a strategy of standardisation should only be applied if a threat or problem the company faces is perceived as solvable in that way, or the company sees greater profit in a standardised approach than in a purely local one (20). Marketing is, in general, said to receive 'high' to 'moderate' degrees of HQ involvement in relation to other management functions. Previous studies have usually grouped finance and research and development (R & D) as tightly centralised, marketing personnel having high to moderate levels of HQ involvement and purchasing as being subject to little HQ involvement (13). Another study indicates that larger MNCs tend not to become involved in affiliates' financial activities but exert control over their marketing (11), the explanation being that exercising financial control over affiliates becomes more difficult as MNCs become larger. Such findings verify the conflicting results obtained when looking at standardising international marketing. It is extremely difficult to come up with generalisations that will hold true in every country and under every circumstance: rather, each piece of research acts as a case study. We will try to categorise these investigations to see whether or not any patterns emerge.

Studies that have investigated the level of standardisation in the marketing functions of the US and European subsidiaries of MNCs report a standardisation of marketing of between 50 and 70% (5, 12, 21). However, other studies conducted in different subsidiary countries, where local managers were interviewed, yield conflicting results. For instance, Garnier *et al.* (19) (examining Mexican affiliates of US-based companies) identify marketing as the most decentralised function among finance, production and personnel. Sim (15), exploring Malaysian subsidiaries of US-, UK- and Japanese-owned parents, groups marketing as under the most decentralised of functions. In the same analysis, finance, ownership and R & D are said to receive most HQ involvement. Even countries at similar levels of development or with similar cultural patterns do not have similar marketing practices (22). Marketing practices differ in different environmental climates. For example, systematic patterns in marketing are only found in companies in Sri Lanka and Japan, but not in Italy, Greece or Chile: high degrees of variation are found in corporates based in these five countries. Garnier *et al.* (19) identify the conditions that lead to a centralisation of marketing as follows:

- A high volume of communications between the affiliate and the HQ.
- Functional or geographical organisational structures adopted.
- An extensive integration of the production processes with other affiliates.
- A higher share of equity by the HQ in the local affiliate's capital.
- Larger perceived differences between the parent-company country and affiliate countries.

Other investigations raise further points. Multiproduct firms organised internationally on product-division lines are less standardised. However, firms with an international division at HQ will be exposed to greater degrees of standardisation (18). In addition, if internal organisation costs are lower, the degree of standardisation applied will be greater. The more interpenetrated the market in larger markets, the higher the standardisation of marketing techniques there will be. Non-uniform marketing programmes are advised in international markets if firms have

- ambitious sales targets and market-share goals;
- operations in many foreign markets;
- extensive financial and managerial resources;
- a global production network; and
- significant joint-venture operations (23).

However, firms with

- less ambitious sales goals;
- a greater emphasis on cost control;
- few production plants; and
- fully owned subsidiaries overseas

can have more widespread standardised strategies.

These studies consider marketing as one item, without going into an analysis of individual marketing-mix elements. In the following sections we wish to concentrate on the degree of standardisation applied to the product, to promotions and, of course, to across-border advertising. However, before proceeding we will take one last look at controlling the 'HQ's control' in marketing to see what is recommended for achieving that end.

Wiechmann (24) suggests 'corporate acculturation' (local managers' training at head office – HO) and 'systems transfer' (uniformity in marketing planning and budgeting in MNCs to simplify communications). In addition, 'people transfer' (enabling short- and long-term contacts between HQ and local management personnel) is recommended as a midway point on the decentralisation–centralisation scale. Nestlé's product management team is, furthermore, given as an example of 'systems transfer' (25). In this solution there is one marketing bible for each brand, which includes the training of product managers, budget planning and approval, systems checks and evaluations, right down to the responsibilities of product managers. Through 'systems transfer' HQs ensure that subsidiaries make use of the same policies without actually policing it themselves. 'Systematic cross-border analysis' before standardisation is also mentioned, mainly because executives are interested in the *process* of standardising marketing programmes, not in the standardisation of marketing programmes itself (21). The Cresap report (5) offers different advice: companies considering changes in their HQ organisation should begin with core tasks and build up as the HQ. Involving operating units in the decision is also mentioned. The implications of organisational change on company staff should, furthermore, be acknowledged by HQs to attain successful results.

POWER OVER GLOBAL PRODUCTS

Having examined HQ involvement in marketing elements, we will now look specifically at the product itself, and the degree to which it is standardised or adapted by subsidiaries. Generally speaking, products are usually standardised rather than adapted by subsidiaries, and choosing the right product to market in a foreign country is of the utmost importance. First of all, they should have the 'appropriate technology' (the World Bank (26) specifies that they should be useful, acceptable and affordable). However, it is very difficult to define the appropriate product, because the criteria applied by consumers, firms and governments are different. However, it is said that entrepreneurial responsibility lies with the firm to create the appropriate product according to the specifications set by the groups involved. Marketers are, therefore, warned of the attractiveness of the product-standardisation concept: 'The simplicity of the idea masks the complexity of implementing it' (27). Standardising products means trading risk and rigidity for improved cost efficiency. Companies are, therefore, advised to think twice before taking on a global product structure. This same note of caution is even extended to the issue of new-product development. It is argued that inventors usually come up with products that are suitable for their own markets; new-product developments can therefore be achieved only by the native entrepreneurs of any local market in accordance with national demand (28).

The foregoing are some of the warnings raised about product standardisation, but it is, however, worthwhile taking a closer look at specific examples. Are products standardised across countries and, if so, to what degree? Are any differences observed in developed and less-developed countries when standardising products across borders? Ward (12), studying 53 US subsidiaries of European-owned companies, notes a 66% adaptation of products for the US market (it should, however, be stressed that this was an investigation mostly carried out on industrial goods, not consumer goods). Ward's findings contradict the long-standing belief that industrial goods are directly transferable across countries. Most adaptations that are made are related to the use or the operation of the product, or its labelling. Styling also tends to have a relative importance for electrical and consumer goods. Another study, which explored the standardisation of US brands, takes the use of the same brand name as a measure of standardisation. Of the brands studied, 86% used the same name in foreign markets as in the USA (29). However, products need not be standard even if they carry the same brand names in different markets. In this study, no relationship was established between the age of the brand and the degree of standardisation applied.

A further investigation that worked with a restricted sample of ten UK bed-linen exporters to six European countries, observed vast variations even in this traditional product group. Adaptations in pillow-case sizes, labelling, design and colour were made by the UK exporters mostly for the French market (30). It was concluded that, as far as bed linens go, it is difficult to regard Europe as one market (such is the state of product standardisation in Western countries)!

If we turn to how less-developed countries (LDCs) cope with product standardisation, we encounter Hill and Still's work on 61 subsidiaries of consumer packaged goods operating in 22 LDCs (31). Hill and Still indicate that, on average, 4.1 changes are made per product in these countries, and only one item in ten is transferred to LDCs without modification. Changes made to the product are categorised in two groups. These are as follows:

- 'Mandatory changes' – such as alterations made to measurement units, packaging sizes and labelling.
- 'Optional changes' – including package aesthetics, product constituents and package protection. These are termed partly optional: wholly optional changes include product features, usage instructions and brand names. Nearly 70% of all changes fall into the 'optional changes' category.

Companies choose to make these changes to strengthen their position in the market because (in LDCs) the MNCs' battle is not against competitors but against the occurrence of likely blunders in local customs and market behaviour. Food, drink and general consumer items are classed as the most likely products to require adaptations. Cosmetics and pharmaceuticals experience less-drastic adaptation patterns (32). When the sample brands included in the study were differentiated as urban and semi-urban, again differences emerged (33). In semi-urban markets, far more adaptations were applied (78 in number) than in urban markets (21 in number). The adaptations made for the semi-urban markets were mostly concerned with packaging protection, product features and labelling.

This last study is significant in that it exhibits intra-country differences in LDCs: not only it is necessary to make certain product adaptations when transferring products from Western countries to LDCs, but marketers should also be sensitive about the changes that might be needed for different market segments within LDCs. This last point once again raises Keegan's comment: 'the more you know about a country, the more you think it is unique' (Chapter 3, reference 2).

STANDARDISE PROMOTIONS ACROSS COUNTRIES, OR ELSE . . .

In time, the promotions employed by the foreign subsidiaries of MNCs become less standardised. For example, Dunn (34) has quantified this phenomenon between the years 1964 and 1970. Companies started to employ international advertising consultants in the 1970s. These consultants would travel around the world to help locals to implement the modifications of a given campaign. However, they would not ask locals to run the prototype campaign. In general, the product and promotion adaptations undertaken depend upon the similarities noted between the home-country market and foreign-subsidiary markets. These adaptations also differ according to how local management perceives the similarities or differences between the home country and their own local market (35). The home office's strength is reflected best in the extent of the changes made in transferred promotional themes. Promotions are generally considered to receive less HQ involvement because sales promotions are 'executive-sensitive elements'. It is, therefore, better if they are left to local management. However, this cannot be said, for example, for product positioning, because such 'strategic elements' are more likely to receive HQ intervention (21).

Numerous authors have attempted to identify the effective promotional strategies used in the different segments of various countries. One such study (36) makes use of product perceptions ('low' and 'high' awareness) and product-attribute preferences. The recommended solution is the execution of a campaign according to the specific needs of each country. Another suggestion is to use a different promotion if the product is purchased for a different reason (37). How the product is used has nothing to do with the promotion strategy, but adaptations in both product and promotions are advised if the product-purchasing reasons and its end-use applications are different. We need to stress here that Littler's suggestion (*ibid.*) comes across as an over-simple view. Is it possible to decide on product and promotion standardisation by looking at two factors only? Is this realistic? Doesn't it deny the complexity of the marketplace and many other elements that affect the final outcome? If international marketing success depends only upon two factors, why do people make such a big issue of it?

The issue of standardising promotions becomes even more complex when LDCs are taken into account. Only one in ten out of 61 LDC subsidiaries makes 80% adaptations in its promotions. A further 46% admit that their adaptations are between 0 and 20% (35). One explanation for this is that MNCs could be targeting their promotions at the better-off urban consumers in LDCs, or that they expect LDC consumers to be more open to foreign-orientated themes. Researchers have also supplied evidence that product and promotion adaptations are not independent events: put simply, adaptation in one triggers adaptation in the other.

Once again, in the data collected from 61 subsidiaries of 19 MNCs drawn from 22 LDCs, the use of sales promotions turns out to be more popular than media (38). Whichever media are widely available are the ones used in subsidiary countries – MNCs cannot be very choosy in this respect. However, sales promotions are company initiated and controlled. Most sales promotions are not affected by environmental factors and they are thus the most preferred. The different media types most popular in different sectors are also differentiated (*ibid.*). It is no secret that the most popular media differ from country to country. However, unorthodox media emerge in LDCs, including the use of loudspeaker trucks, mobile films, riverboats with speakers, and the like, for reaching remote rural parts (39). Similarly, Coca Cola's free-dress give-away campaign from years ago is still well known (40). These dresses had Coke bottles colourfully printed on them in indelible ink. They were made for African countries, where press and TV advertising in those days was not very effective.

Even the promotional techniques used in the urban and semi-urban segments of LDCs are not the same. As different targets they have dissimilar requirements and needs. Generally, 'soft-sell' promotions are preferred in urban areas, but 'hard-sell' promotions are more widespread in suburban and in rural areas. In urban programmes, print media are more apparent, but of a sudden, vocally orientated media (such as TV and radio) surfaced in urban/suburban activities (39). These examples confirm that the media types used are far from standard when compared to other marketing-mix elements, and the points raised emphasise how MNCs and LDCs interact. They also accentuate how technology transfer affects the culture of LDCs, where social norms, values and customs might be different. It should also be borne in mind that the composite elements of culture are given different levels of importance in each country. MNCs must first master these nuances to understand and evaluate the different approaches to be utilised in various countries when running promotion campaigns. 'One sight, one sound, one sell' has, therefore, far too many implications in subsidiary countries than ever imagined.

STANDARDISE ADVERTISING CAMPAIGNS, OR ELSE ...

Not many studies have looked into the standardisation of advertising. This area is generally covered when product and promotion standardisation observed between the HQ and its subsidiaries is examined. Ones specifically devised to scrutinise HQ involvement in subsidiaries' advertising activities when running smooth global campaigns are rather scarce.

We will first look at whether or not MNCs know where their advertising budgets are being spent. A study undertaken by Dunn (41) examines the types of research used by MNCs to measure advertising efforts in Western Europe and the Middle East. These MNCs are those that allocate larger and larger advertising budgets every year. The results highlight soap and detergent companies as the big spenders on advertising research. Pharmaceuticals, on the other hand, are identified as using less research conducted on their advertising copies. In a nutshell, it is not wrong to conclude that, although MNCs are allocating huge advertising budgets, they do not copy search their advertising. The ones that do search are limited to a few companies and agencies. It is important to add that the MNCs and agencies that were examined are active in at least four foreign markets and cover a variety of products.

Another study analysed successful/unsuccessful campaigns and reached a similar verdict (42). This verdict was that agencies do not set objectives or know about their campaigns' successes even though these campaigns are considered publicly to be successful! Britt's findings (*ibid.*) are rather amusing and deserve further attention. The study covers 135 successful campaigns created by 40 US agencies, with the aim of comparing agencies' replies on 'campaign objectives' with 'proofs of success of the campaign'. The results obtained can be classified as follows:

1. Whether or not the measurable objectives given by agencies were specific enough. The observed deficiencies in responses were
   - measurable objectives not stated (99%);
   - not realising that advertising results cannot be measured in sales (24%);
   - not identifying the audience (16%); and
   - the use of superlatives, which are not measurable (2%).
2. Whether or not the agencies tried to measure the campaign's effectiveness according to previously set objectives. Measures used were not related to objectives in 70% of responses. This was mainly because
   - the objective given was awareness, measured in sales;
   - the objective given was new image, measured in readership; and
   - more than one objective was stated; success was measured in relation only to one of the objectives.
3. Whether or not the responses given changed according to the agency size and the product group. Bigger agencies generally stated objectives and afterwards measured them more often. No trend was observed in different product groups.

These findings definitely make one wonder about the justification of large sums of money being spent on advertising without knowing how and why.

Two other complementary studies need to be mentioned here about how advertising agencies (43) and advertisers (44) evaluate successful campaigns. These studies are not as realistic as the previous work and are even a little Utopian. To begin with, the authors take the success of a campaign as the unknown, and limit its measurement to three elements: awareness, attitude change and sales. They then name a second set of unknowns (variables, if you prefer it) and call them factors affecting successful campaigns. These are

- product characteristics;
- competition;
- managerial and financial resources;
- agent-client relationship;
- market research efforts;
- nature of market;
- message positioning and creativity; and
- media selection.

Their results point out that campaigns that fulfil successful advertising criteria receive adequate financial and managerial resources and they are based on careful media planning. There is a match between product attributes and consumer needs. They use messages that are unique and creative. However, the presence of competition and problematic agency–client relationships have negative effects on the success of the campaign. No one can deny the importance of these factors on the final outcome of any advertising campaign. It would be total bliss if advertisers and agencies played the game with those conditions fulfilled, but the truth is that, unfortunately (or fortunately), they do not. If they did, they would no longer have any worries about beating their competitors in this deadly game. That is why these two studies were described as a little Utopian, because they are far from being a simulation of real-market conditions. In the marketplace, players experience unfairness, set-backs, booms, mediocre ads, great ads, lousy ads or blessings. They become winners and losers, and this is what makes business life so exciting and rewarding. Business is not conducted in a vacuum, and it shouldn't be, either. Researchers, therefore, should be prepared to take a broader view, a view closer to the real life of business – otherwise the results cannot be put into practice one way or another.

Looking at the problem from a different perspective, three groups of factors are listed that affect the decision to transfer campaigns: market (economic), cultural and media factors (45). Market factors were found to receive most attention among US advertisers before advertising campaigns were transferred. However, a more balanced view is recommended when assessing a campaign's transferability across borders. All three factors should be taken into account, rather than just the economic. Similarly, in a checklist developed to evaluate a campaign's transferability,

- consumption patterns (such as purchase and usage patterns);
- psychological characteristics (such as attitudes towards the product/service and the brand); and
- cultural criteria

are included in the grid (46). It is also emphasised here that no research has ever incorporated psychological and cultural factors into the smooth transfer of global campaigns. Even if market and economic factors yield positive results they do not guarantee the success of the campaign. If cultural and psychological factors are not favourable, advertising can easily fail.

In order to be able to visualise the extent and dimensions of HQ involvement in subsidiary advertising activities, one or two figures are desirable. One study that included US non-durable firms' international advertising managers revealed that 90% employ some form of standardised advertising (47). However, this added straight away that, in only 17% of the companies interviewed, more than 50% of the total advertising was standardised. Managers assign less importance to cultural differences than would be expected. In addition, they are sceptical about a heavy reliance on the standardised approach.

In an article complementary to this, the question was asked about which kind of corporate is more suitable for global advertising (48). The relationship between the local advertising manager's degree of autonomy (as centralised/ decentralised) and where the advertising agency is based (as a US/foreign-based agency) is examined. The more centralised companies emerge as being the ones more suitable for global advertising. Companies that are less concerned about cultural differences and that work with a US-based agency are also more suitable for running international campaigns.

In these studies, advertising was considered as one item. However, more recent investigations split advertising into its components and look at each component's degree of standardisation in relation to the others. One such piece of research was carried out on 28 non-randomly selected MNCs with HQs in the Cleveland–Akron–Pittsburg industrial triangle (49). The four international advertising decisions considered were establishing objectives, the budget, creative strategy and media decisions. HQ involvement was found to be higher in planning and control decisions. Establishing advertising objectives and budgets were also placed in this group. However, strategy areas are subject to less HQ intervention. Creative strategy and media selection are examples of such decisions. HQs might become involved in international media-selection decisions. For creative strategy, HQs generally monitor and, sometimes, give final approval, but they do not go beyond that. It is also forecast that the control of advertising strategy and evaluation will become more centralised in the early 1990s. HQ involvement in the execution of advertising is also expected to become more decentralised during the same period (50).

Killough (51), reviewing 120 product and services' advertising campaigns, interviewed 65 senior managers in MNCs and in international advertising agencies. His sample includes consumer products (60%), capital-intensive products (25%) and services (15%). The factors that affect the success or failure of campaigns across borders are investigated. The key element in successful transfers was identified as a strong commitment to planning *per se*. What is more, highly centralised strategic planning is needed that will (at the same time) allow flexibility in executional interpretation at the local level. A total of 50% of the executives interviewed believed firmly that buying propositions can be transferred without much change. When it came to the use of the same creative presentation, this only held true for less than 30% of all campaigns.

The final recommendation is to set up a global creative team. This team should be brought together at the beginning of production. They should work together and develop consciously a campaign that will minimise barriers in creative advertising. The final campaign might change from market to market, but the goal should be to produce 'moduli'. Therefore 'moduli' cannot be defined. It could be that a buying proposition or a visual hook will stay the same in every market the campaign is run. This is a practical suggestion that enables the standardisation of advertising strategy while, at the same time, giving autonomy to local management in the execution of the campaign.

This sounds like a sensible solution, but can we speak of economies of scale achieved in production costs, in manpower and in time? We will see whether or not the London agency executives who were interviewed came up with a better answer than this in Chapter 9. The art is to create campaigns that look locally produced in every market without having to create or produce individual advertising campaigns for each market. In this way one could talk about cost effectiveness without being stamped as 'foreign' in every market in which the campaign is shown. Compromise campaigns look foreign and are never right – not even in the markets where they were produced!

Finally, another study that was conducted on US-based MNCs' international advertising executives reports conflicting findings. The results were based on 34 questionnaires (with a response rate of 23%) submitted to both industrial and consumer-product marketers. Three sets of factors are given (52):

- Guiding variables, including target markets and product positioning.
- Strategy variables, which are campaign objectives, campaign theme and media objectives.
- Tactical variables covering basic media mix, media schedules, visual creative execution and copy.

A high degree of standardisation was noted in these three factors. If strategy variables are standardised, then so are guiding variables. Differing from other studies, this research reports a high standardisation of visual creative executions. An interpretation of this rather surprising finding goes something like the following. The visuals used might be serving as the theme of the advertising campaign. Hence, as it is desirable to standardise campaign themes, visual executions end up being the same as well. This study gives no evidence of higher standardisation observed in firms with similar product usages around the world. Although it is difficult to believe, no significant differences were reported regarding the standardisation of any advertising-related factors in more centralised firms.

Another study emphasises country-specific differences in advertising standardisation across MNC subsidiaries (53). The researchers, who studied Canadian, US, Japanese and European firms, isolate Canadian firms as the most centralised in their advertising activities. A total of 43% of Canadian firms have their advertising produced by their HQs. The same statistic is 25% for European companies, 15% for US firms and 13% for the Japanese.

To conclude this section with a practical guideline, we include a useful generalisation for effective marketing and advertising standardisation. It was developed and used by the McCann-Erickson Agency. The agency's broad categorisation is that marketing standardisation works best (54, p. 249) when the brand

- is contemporary, international and fashion orientated;
- is marketed at similar price levels to similar audiences;
- has similar consumption patterns;
- is younger or youth orientated; and
- is an indulgence product rather than a necessity.

Moreover, advertising centralisation works best when the campaign

- has a strong creative idea;

- is image orientated or product performance orientated;
- is not dependent on price or promotion;
- avoids local personalities, models or slogans; and
- has a strong 'brand property'.

WHAT PREVIOUS STUDIES HAVE COVERED AND THE ULTIMATE AIM OF THIS BOOK

Put simply, previous research studies have yielded contradictory results, be it research conducted on standardisation applied to marketing-mix elements or standardisation employed in subsidiary advertising activities. Additionally, in most cases standardisation applied to advertising is examined within the context of other marketing-mix elements. Therefore advertising does not receive enough attention and is not analysed thoroughly. Advertising consists of different elements: from media selection to the actual production of a campaign, its copy, its execution, advertising legislation, the length of the commercial, and the setting or approving of advertising budgets. Hence, the degree of standardisation applied to 'advertising' does not mean much by itself, because it is not possible to identify which particular element of the advertising respondents are referring to when answering general questions. Studies have attempted to answer very general questions as far as advertising standardisation in subsidiaries is concerned – and advertising is too wide an area to receive such scant attention.

Furthermore, in studies where data was collected through postal questionnaires, very low response rates are reported: 5.1% in Garnier *et al.* (19); and 14% in Rosen, Boddewyn and Louis (29). The highest response rate achieved was by Donnelly and Ryans (47) with 40%.

Generally speaking, these studies comprise small samples (usually 25–30 interviews). Some are selected through a non-random sampling method, for example, being confined to a particular geographical area (such as Wills and Ryans (49)). Killough (51), however, interviewed 65 top executives in MNCs and agencies, and Sorenson and Wiechmann (21) interviewed over 100 executives in 27 MNCs. In addition, some of this research does not concentrate on one specific respondent group, such as advertisers or agencies or media executives. Instead they include in these small samples of 25–30 interviews executives with different titles in different parts of the world. (Griffin (50) covers four groups with a sample of 33; Dunn (41) draws conclusions from 30 advertisers, 10 agencies and 6 market research firms.) The findings often prove to be inconclusive or, at best, to yield statistically not significant results, mainly because they were conducted on a mixture of respondents, with diverse aims and goals.

Another common mistake is to make comparisons with previous research, to look at different response groups and to use different sets of variables. The executives interviewed in these studies generally over-emphasise their own power and role, whether they are based at HQs or in subsidiaries. Therefore studies that have worked with a sample of local marketing executives report higher degrees of adaptation employed in advertising activities. On the other hand, research undertaken to collect data from HQ marketing executives reports a shift towards centralised decision-making in international advertising activities. Dunn (34) and Keegan, Still and Hill (35) also point to this contradiction. For example, Ryans and Ratz (52) describe a tendency towards centralisation in their study of US-based MNCs. Aydin and Terpstra (17) conclude that low degrees of marketing know-how are transferred from HQs to 28 Turkish subsidiaries. Garnier *et al.* (19), in a similar study of Mexican affiliates, state that these affiliates enjoy a high degree of autonomy.

Moreover, it is not possible to split the samples in these studies because the samples employed are small. As most statistical techniques require large samples to work with, a sample of 30 covering 4 product groups means approximately 7 cases from each sector. No statistical test result with a sample size of 7 will be reliable, even if the test produces results. Therefore, the different trends exhibited by differently split groups (such as food products being subject to a decentralised approach, whereas cosmetics receive more centralisation) are conclusions based on smaller samples. Researchers provide their own perceptions and subjective evaluations of differently split groups with regard to the degree of standardisation applied to these various split groups.

However, these are not our only worries: other authors have expressed a concern about the lack of dependable and consistent information on international advertising. Britt (55, p. 293) puts it bluntly as follows:

> To date no method of research on cultural and psychological factors has been developed to ascertain the potential for advertising standardisation for a given product or service.
>
> It must be remembered that little or nothing exists at present to aid the marketing and advertising executive in his decision-making on this vital matter.

It is also pointed out that international advertising and marketing are still largely practised on a pragmatic basis. Little empirical research has been done in this area, and this is not definitive, either (56). Ryans and Ratz (52), agreeing with the others, suggest the use of larger samples and more in-depth studies in future research. They add that previous studies do not acknowledge the different component dimensions of international advertising and that they do not recognise the wide range of decisions that fall into this area. Their advice to researchers, therefore, is to consider all the relevant elements of international advertising as well as to attempt to break down in a similar fashion other marketing-mix elements to their components. This particular study was positioned by taking into account all the aforementioned shortcomings of previous work. The aim was not to make the same mistakes. Rather, the intention was to build on previous research by making use of the points raised and the suggestions made by other researchers.

Certain points need to be clarified first about this study. The findings reported in the present book (Chapters 6–10) are part of a larger study conducted among both UK subsidiaries of MNCs as advertisers, and among UK branches of international advertising agencies (57). The original study, therefore, comprises two relatively large samples. The first is the advertisers' sample (as agencies' clients). It consists of 399 brands drawn from 143 UK subsidiaries of foreign-owned companies that market fast-moving consumer goods (FMCGs) and some services. The parent companies' homes are represented by 19 countries and they cover 20 sectors. As this was such a large sample, the statistical tests that were conducted even on the split groups of the sample yielded reliable results. Because the advertisers' sample included 399 brand managers, the data was collected through postal questionnaires. A high, valid, response rate of 29% was obtained from these. The returned questionnaires were analysed using the Statistical Package for Social Sciences (SPSS-X). We inevitably ended up with quantitative results. The results obtained from the advertisers in the study are not included here: if the readership of this book was to be the practitioner, we wanted to stay away from the academic. Even a brief mention of SPSS-X would attract only those who are struggling with the package!

Having stated what is not in this book, it is now time to describe what is included. The information obtained from agency executives based in the UK offices of international advertising agencies are reported. In total, 33 contacts were obtained from 13 international advertising agencies, covering 39 accounts in the agency sample. Industrial goods are not included in the study in order to concentrate on FMCGs, as these are intensively distributed and frequently purchased. Advertising is both necessary and economic for those products in order to maintain the high brand profiles needed for marketplace success (38). In the agency sample, information was gathered with the help of personal interviews. The findings obtained from the agencies are, therefore, qualitative in nature. To retain the authenticity of these interviews, direct quotations from these talks are used abundantly in the following chapters. It is believed they make the reading easier, as well as expressing ideas more effectively. (The research methodology employed, how the research was conducted, how agencies were selected and contacted are explained thoroughly in Appendix I. The questionnaires used while collecting the data are included in Appendix II.)

To recap, this book aims specifically at examining HO involvement in the advertising activities of international brands through the eyes of international agency executives. It was the intention to identify the preconditions necessary for the smooth transfer of international campaigns across countries, particularly to the UK. The in-depth interviews conducted with London agency executives lay stress specifically on smooth international agency and client relationships as the basis for successful transnational campaigns.

THE CURRENT ISSUES RAISED

Having now discussed the frequently used concepts of advertising, and having reviewed advocates' and opponents' views on global advertising and looked into the HQ's role, influence and even intervention in advertising, should have helped us in a number of ways. First, it refreshed our memories: we are now more aware of the current state of the debate on globalisation. We know each camp's strengths and weaknesses. You may have already decided in which camp you see yourself. These preceding pages also helped us to detect unanswered questions in this area. We will attempt now a shot at these knotty questions, for this is the challenge the book faces. We aim to answer the questions listed below in order to understand better HO involvement in the international advertising activities of international advertising agencies and international brands:

1. What is the ratio of international accounts receiving 'high' and 'low' HO involvement in their advertising activities?
2. What are the characteristics of 'high' and 'low' involvement accounts in international advertising agencies?
3. What is the nature of agency HO involvement? When does it escalate? When does it ease?
4. What is the essence of the international agency–client relationship? How could the agency–client paradox be solved?
5. What is the organisational structure adopted in global campaigns? Does it have any effect on the smooth transfer of campaigns?
6. What type(s) of advertising are more suitable in global advertising practices?
7. What do agency executives feel about global campaigns?
8. What is the relationship between the successful standardisation of marketing-mix elements and transferring global campaigns?
9. How is 'successful' advertising defined by agency executives? What was the extent of the use of the DAGMAR model among practitioners at the end of the 1980s?
10. Is there any relationship between different ways of developing global campaigns and the clients' corporate culture?
11. What are the relative degrees of adaptation employed in the individual elements of advertising campaigns transferred to the UK?
12. How will the new media affect global campaigns? How do agency executives react to the new media?
13. What are the preconditions that enable advertisers and agencies to succeed in smooth global campaign transfers across countries?

These questions are certainly varied and intricate. I hope you will also feel that they are answered as you read through the remaining pages of this book. Nonetheless, I guarantee you will find it amusing. *Bon appétit*!

REFERENCES

1. Keegan, W. J. (1988) Global competition: strategic alternatives (paper presented at the Academy of International Management Conference), San Diego, Calif. October.

2. Thorelli, H. B. (1973) 'Introduction' and 'International marketing: an ecologic view', in H. B. Thorelli (ed.) *International Marketing Strategy*, Penguin Books, Harmondsworth, pp. 11–39.
3. Terpstra, V. (1987) The evolution of international marketing, *International Marketing Review*, Summer, pp. 47–59.
4. Skapinker, M. (1988) Justifying their varied existence, *The Financial Times*, 1 July, p. 20.
5. *The Effective Head Office* (1988) compiled by Cresap, sponsored by the British Institute of Management, Corby.
6. Bodinat, H. (1974) Multinational decentralisation: doomed if you do, doomed if you don't, *European Business*, Summer, pp. 64–70.
7. Hamel, G. and Prahalad, C. K. (1985) Do you really have a global strategy? *Harvard Business Review*, July/August, pp. 139–48.
8. Goold, M. and Campbell, A. (1987) *Strategies and Styles: The Role of the Centre in Managing Diversified Corporations*, Blackwell, Oxford.
9. Keegan, W. J. (1973) Headquarters involvement in multinational marketing, in H. B. Thorelli (ed.) *International Marketing Strategy*, Penguin Books, Harmondsworth, pp. 283–9 (originally published in *Columbia Journal of World Business*, Vol. 6, no. 1, 1971, pp. 85–90).
10. Keegan, W. J. (1972) Multinational marketing control, *Journal of International Business Studies*, Vol. 3, no. 2, Fall, pp. 33–47.
11. Gates, S. R. and Egelhoff, W. G. (1986) Centralization in headquarters – subsidiary relationships, *Journal of International Business Studies*, Vol. XVII, no. 1, Summer, pp. 71–92.
12. Ward, J. J. (1973) Product and promotion adaptation by European firms in the US, *Journal of International Business Studies*, Vol. 4, no. 1, Spring, pp. 79–85.
13. Wiechmann, U. E. (1976) *Marketing Management in Multinational Firms – The Consumer Packaged Goods Industry*, Praeger, New York, NY.
14. Quelch, J. A. and Hoff, E. J. (1986) Customizing global marketing, *Harvard Business Review*, Vol. 64, no. 3, May/June, pp. 56–9.
15. Sim, A. B. (1979) Decentralised management of subsidiaries and their performance, *Management International Review*, Vol. 17, no. 2, pp. 45–51.
16. Going global (1986) *European Management Journal*, Vol. 4, no. 1, Spring, pp. 10–28.
17. Aydin, N. and Terpstra, V. (1981) Marketing know-how transfers by multinationals: a case study in Turkey, *Journal of International Business Studies*, Vol. XII, no. 3, Winter, pp. 35–48.
18. Rau, I. A. and Preble, J. F. (1987) Standardisation of marketing strategy by multinationals, *International Marketing Review*, Autumn, pp. 18–28.
19. Garnier, G., Osborn, T. N., Galicia, F. and Lecon, R. (1979) Autonomy of the Mexican affiliates of US multinational corporations, *Columbia Journal of World Business*, Spring, pp. 78–90.
20. Sands, S. (1979) Can you standardise international marketing strategy? *Journal of the Academy of Marketing Science*, Vol. 7, no. 1/2, Winter/Spring, pp. 117–34.
21. Sorenson, R. Z. and Wiechmann U. E. (1975) How multinationals view marketing standardization, *Harvard Business Review*, Vol. 53, May/June, pp. 38–44, 48–50, 54, 166–7.
22. Douglas, S. P. and Wind, Y. (1973) Environmental factors and marketing practices, *European Journal of Marketing*, Vol. 7, no. 3, Autumn, pp. 155–65.
23. Walters, P. G. P. (1986) International marketing policy: a discussion of the standardization construct and its relevance for corporate policy, *Journal of International Business Studies*, Summer, pp. 55–69.
24. Wiechmann, U. E. (1979) Integrating multinational marketing activities, in S. W. Dunn and E. S. Lorimor (eds.) *International Advertising and Marketing*, Grid

Publications, Columbus, Ohio, pp. 27–41 (originally published in *Columbia Journal of World Business*, Winter, 1974, pp. 7–16).
25. d'Antin, P. (1971) The Nestlé product manager as demigod, *European Business*, no. 28, Spring, pp. 44–9.
26. Terpstra, V. (1981) On marketing appropriate products in developing countries, *Journal of International Marketing*, Vol. 1, no. 1, pp. 3–15.
27. Davidson, W. H. and Haspeslagh, P. (1982) Shaping a global product organization, *Harvard Business Review*, July/August, pp. 125–32.
28. Wells, L. T. jr (1968) A product life-cycle for international trade, *Journal of Marketing*, Vol. 32, pp. 1–6.
29. Rosen, B. N., Boddewyn, J. J. and Louis, E. A. (1989) US brands abroad: an empirical study on global branding, *International Marketing Review*, Vol. 6, no. 1, pp. 7–19.
30. Whitelock, J. M. (1987) Global marketing and the case for international product standardisation, *European Journal of Marketing*, Vol. 21, no. 9, pp. 32–44.
31. Hill, J. S. and Still, R. R. (1984) Adapting products to LDC tastes, *Harvard Business Review*, March/April, pp. 92–101.
32. Still, R. R. and Hill, J. S. (1984) Adapting consumer products to lesser-developed markets, *Journal of Business Research*, Vol. 12, pp. 51–61.
33. Hill, J. S. and Still, R. R. (1984) Effects of urbanization on multinational product planning: markets in lesser-developed countries, *Columbia Journal of World Business*, Summer, pp. 62–7.
34. Dunn, S. W. (1976) Effect of national identity on multinational promotional strategy in Europe, *Journal of Marketing*, Vol. 40, no. 4, October, pp. 50–7.
35. Keegan, W. J., Still, R. R. and Hill, J. S. (1987) Transferability and adaptability of products and promotion themes in multinational marketing – MNCs in LDCs, *Journal of Global Marketing*, Vol. 1, nos. 1–2, Fall/Winter, pp. 85–103.
36. Colvin, M., Heeler, R. and Thorpe, J. (1980) Developing international advertising strategy, *Journal of Marketing*, Fall, pp. 73–9.
37. Littler, D. (1984) *Marketing and Product Development*, Philip Allan Publishers (Industrial Studies Series), Oxford, p. 247.
38. Hill, J. S. and Boya, Ü. O. (1987) Consumer goods promotions in developing countries, *International Journal of Advertising*, Vol. 6, pp. 249–64.
39. Hill, J. S. (1984) Targeting promotion in lesser developed countries: a study of multinational corporation strategies, *Journal of Advertising*, Vol. 13, no. 4, pp. 39–48.
40. Mazze, E. M. (1964) How to push a body abroad without making it a corpse, *Business Abroad and Export Trade*, 10 August, pp. 14–16.
41. Dunn, S. W. (1965) Cross-cultural research by US corporations, *Journalism Quarterly*, Summer, pp. 42, 454–7.
42. Britt, S. H. (1976) Are so-called successful advertising campaigns really successful? in R. D. Michman and D. W. Jugenheimer (eds.) *Strategic Advertising Decisions*, Grid Publications, Columbus, Ohio, pp. 119–29 (originally published in *Journal of Advertising Research*, Vol. 9, June 1969, pp. 3–9).
43. Korgaonkar, P. K., Moschis, G. P. and Bellenger, D. N. (1984) Correlates of successful advertising campaigns, *Journal of Advertising Research*, Vol. 24, no. 1, pp. 47–53.
44. Korgaonkar, P. K. and Bellenger, D. N. (1985) Correlates of successful advertising campaigns: the manager's perspective, *Journal of Advertising Research*, Vol. 25, no. 4, pp. 34–9.
45. Dunn, S. W. (1966) The case study approach in cross-cultural research, *Journal of Marketing Research*, Vol. 3, February, pp. 26–31.
46. Britt, S. H. (1974) Standardizing marketing for the international market, *Columbia Journal of World Business*, Winter, pp. 39–45.

47. Donnelly, J. H. jr and Ryans, J. K. jr (1969) Standardized global advertising: a call as yet unanswered, *Journal of Marketing*, Vol. 33, April, pp. 57–60.
48. Donnelly, J. H. jr (1970) Marketing notes and communications, *Journal of Marketing*, Vol. 34, July, pp. 60–3.
49. Wills, J. R. jr and Ryans, J. K. jr (1977) An analysis of headquarters executive involvement in international advertising, *European Journal of Marketing*, Vol. 11, no. 8, pp. 577–84.
50. Griffin, T. (1985) International advertising in the 1990s, in S. Shaw, L. Sparks and E. Kaynak (eds.) *Marketing in the 1990s and Beyond* (Second World Marketing Congress Proceedings, Marketing Education Group, 28–31 August), University of Stirling, Vol. II, pp. 622–31.
51. Killough, J. (1978) Improved payoffs from transnational advertising, *Harvard Business Review*, July/August, pp. 102–10.
52. Ryans, J. K. jr and Ratz, D. G. (1987) Advertising standardisation: a re-examination, *International Journal of Advertising*, Vol. 6, pp. 145–58.
53. Kirpalani, V. H., Laroche, M. and Darmon, R. Y. (1988) Role of headquarter control by multinationals in international advertising decisions, *International Journal of Advertising*, Vol. 7, pp. 323–33.
54. Gilligan, C. and Hird, M. (1986) *International Marketing: Strategy and Management*, Croom Helm, London.
55. Britt, S. H. (1980) Standardising advertising for the international market, in S. Broadbent (ed.) *Market Researchers Look at Advertising*, ESOMAR, London, pp. 292–7 (originally published in CONGRESS: ESOMAR/WAPOR, Quality in Research Special Groups, New York, 1975, pp. 683–98).
56. Lorimor, E. S. (1979) A look at some current articles in international advertising and marketing, in S. W. Dunn and E. S. Lorimor (eds.) *International Advertising and Marketing*, Grid Publications, Columbus, Ohio, pp. 55–66.
57. Vardar, N. (1989) Management of international advertising: involvement of foreign HQs in UK subsidiaries and agencies (PhD thesis), Manchester School of Management, UMIST.

6
BIG BROTHER: THE AGENCY HEAD OFFICE (AHO) OR THE CLIENT'S HQ?

As was mentioned briefly at the end of Chapter 5, the data on international advertising agencies was collected through personally administered interviews. These contacts were all made in the international advertising agencies' London offices. These agencies were chosen, whenever possible, if they had head offices (HOs) outside the UK. (The data-collection method employed is covered in Appendix I.) In total, 13 international advertising agencies were contacted, and the information included in the book is based on 39 international accounts, gathered from 33 account executives in the 13 agencies. Although it was the intention to interview account executives in these agencies, in some cases personnel had differing titles, such as account supervisors or account managers. In others, account directors, international account executives, international account directors or co-ordinators were interviewed, depending on the nature of the account.

One of the objectives in writing this book was to examine international agency–client relationships in successfully transferable global campaigns. Therefore to begin with, the extent of agency head office (AHO) involvement in the UK advertising activities of international accounts represented by the UK branches of international agencies are explored. More specifically, we intend to look at successfully transferable global campaigns across countries from the point of view of London branches of international advertising agencies. Having identified successful campaigns, we describe the extent of AHO involvement in these brands and the degree of standardisation applied to their marketing-mix elements. In addition, the elements of successful campaigns, and how they are adapted to the UK market, are examined. Campaign elements adapted to the UK market and the degree of adaptation applied to these elements are related once more to the extent of AHO involvement. The questionnaires used during these interviews are included in Appendix II. The aim of all the questions was to be able to identify and isolate the factors that affect positively international agency–client relationships while transferring campaigns. By looking at examples of successful campaigns, we believe we will be able to demonstrate certain patterns that might help others who are thinking of establishing such relationships, or those who are trying to improve their existing relationships. Therefore AHO involvement and, more particularly, the AHO role in successfully transferred advertisements is explored in the remaining part of the book.

Since the aim was to look at AHO involvement in global advertising practices, agencies were asked about the extent of their HO's involvement. Interestingly, account executives invariably mentioned their clients' headquarters (HQs) first, instead of their own HOs. This seemed, initially, a mere coincidence. However, as the interviews conducted grew in number, it became apparent that it was actually incorrect to dwell on HO involvement in agencies by itself: the extent of involvement they received from their HOs was very much determined by their clients' corporate culture. And the corporate culture was best displayed by the clients' organisational structure. The way clients organised themselves and their affiliates affected the extent of company HQ involvement. Company HQ involvement would be exerted on their own affiliates and indirectly on their agencies. Figure 6.1 shows the agency–client organisation in its most simplified form; however, it is crucial to be able to visualise how they interact.

At this point it is important to note that these clients are major world advertisers: they allocate huge advertising budgets to their worldwide marketing activities. An account director at Ogilvy & Mather (O & M) put it:

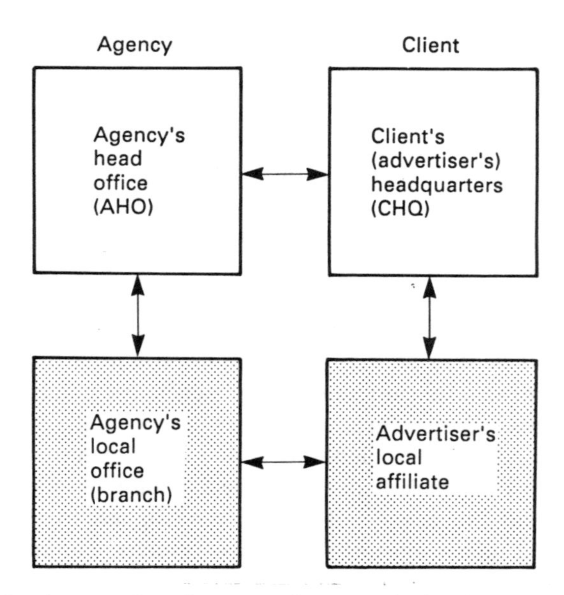

Figure 6.1 A simple representation of agency–client organisational structures

They are one of our biggest clients. They are a huge client to any agency, even probably we have only 15% of their worldwide business. Even with that percent, they come within the top three or four of our worldwide accounts. [However] they probably spend less than about a tenth of 1% of their outgoings on advertising. Advertising is a thousandth of their business. We cannot change that company, but can only understand it and work around the parameters that are set for us. We can advise, but cannot change, nor impose on them.

On the other hand, it needs to be emphasised here that the agencies interviewed had, on average, UK annual billings of £130 million. Therefore they could not be considered as small corporations by any measure. However, they apparently valued their clients and wanted to satisfy them fully, like any other service industry.

THE AGENCY–CLIENT PARADOX

Before looking at HO involvement in agencies, certain aspects of the agency–client relationship need to be discussed. Agency–client relationships have never remained static: clients and agencies undergo metamorphoses at certain times, remodelling and reorganising themselves accordingly. Therefore the relationship has constantly evolved and has, in the long run, eventually been transformed into a new bond. This study shows that clients were the initiators of any change taking place within their own organisation as well as in the agency's. Inevitably each restructuring inflicted certain transfigurations on the agency–client relationship.

An account director from Young & Rubicam (Y & R) expressed this as follows:

No matter which agency or client you talk to, you will always find that the agency will mimic the client's requirements. So the agency is always flexible. International accounts all lie on a continuum between highly centralised and highly decentralised. Our agency is full of clients at both extremes. Even the same clients oscillate between the two, time and time again. It is like a pendulum. It swings. It depends on the state that the client is in, kinds of things they are trying to achieve with their business, the kind of business strategies that they are adopting. Top managers' personalities is what it almost totally depends upon. Basically it is all a reflection of what top management decides to do, how they want to control, which cultural factors cross borders.

An account supervisor of BBDO expressed it thus:

The cultural truth of companies is harder to find out about, because people would not talk freely about it. They will explain it in terms of more logical, rational things like location of offices. Understanding the culture, the way the game is played, corporate beliefs are very very important. To make things more complicated, these rules change every time a new managing director is appointed. Organisational charts can take you so far in understanding the reality. But to have an understanding of corporate culture from our point of view is essential, because it is really what it is all about. Therefore we say to our clients that our organisation and structure will reflect your culture. It is important for us to know what kind of people you are. So that we can decide we are the right people to work with you. Otherwise we will be misleading each other.

Account executives agreed that two clients are never the same. P. Axten – International Co-ordinator of Esso at McCann-Erickson – summarised it as follows: 'You have to start by saying every client is different, either because they are structured or their expectations from the agency are different'.

An account manager at Y & R said the following:

> Some clients have highly organised, disciplined, talented marketing teams. So they require relatively little from us. Other clients will not have any form of marketing discipline, then we have to provide that input. So it does entirely depend on the client. Yet we generally come in line with their procedures. We are a service industry. Yes, we are here to produce great ads, but we are also here to satisfy the customers. They are our food and drink.

Peter Wilken, the Account Director of the Shell account at O & M, gives the following explanation of the client's influence in agency–client relationships. It is taken from P. Wilken's letter to the author, written to give consent to be quoted:

> The Agency does not advocate a universal approach to international client–agency relationships, although the principles of Ogilvy good business practice are common. Centralised clients like American Express require a more centrally controlled agency structure than less centralised clients like Shell. There is no right or wrong way of doing things – what suits one client organisation or agency may not suit another, all good commonsense stuff.

P. Nelson – Unilever Edible Fats International Co-ordinator at McCann-Erickson – indicated that even within the same corporate umbrella some lines of business adopt a more centralised approach in their advertising activities than others. For example, in Unilever, the edible-fats division might be highly decentralised. On the other hand, for their toiletry brands, they might transfer advertising campaigns across borders. It was, therefore, not just one approach for each client that the agency faced: it was more likely to be meeting the requirements of individual brands. In order to be able to accommodate this, agencies need to be very flexible.

We will now look at how far agencies go to be flexible. The following quotations are taken from various account executives to highlight the influence agencies are subject to from clients. These also indicate how agencies replicate clients' structures, according to clients' needs.

A. Gledhill (Account Director of TWA, Y & R) pointed out that 'The only way to do it is to mirror [the structure] of client's organisation. Otherwise we have repeatedly found out that you are working in variance with their natural ways, which is not cost-effective'.

Another executive from O & M elaborated the same point with a few vivid examples:

> Our client separated the UK from the rest of Europe, because they had two people whom they wanted to promote as regional executives! So they classified UK as one region and promoted both men as regional executives. The problem started with the agency though, because the team here is still the same team. Splitting ourselves wasn't that easy, but we have split ourselves, too!

> We have a very similar structure to theirs, to make sure they find their counterparts in every market.
>
> For our client direct response is crucial. So we are trying to improve ourselves on that. We have a supportive team dealing only with direct response. We are trying to make sure, whatever service we give, it is a fully orchestrated one.

R. Steward – Unilever Frozen Products International Co-ordinator at McCann-Erickson – said 'We have a shadow of each other'.

F. Clementis of Foote Cone & Belding (FCB) (Europe), International Account Executive for Colgate Palmolive, expressed this by saying 'One of the reasons why we decided to set up a European co-ordination system was because of our client. It is very much client-led'. Yet another account co-ordinator from McCann's pointed out that 'Their [client's] organisation is massive and to be able to match it, you need to start it there and move it around theirs'.

P. Nelson of McCann's gave another example of how they reflect the client's set-up within their own agency:

> The Unilever Advertising Co-ordinator has no line authority over his operating companies. He is a consultant and an adviser. Likewise, I have no line authority over other agency offices in this account.
>
> It is also a matching of responsibilities. I am the same person, but I did entirely different jobs in three different accounts. Primary concern in all these different accounts is the management structure, because it dictates the degree to which the advertising executions can be controlled in local situations.

K. Rubie (Europe and Middle East Regional Managing Director of Leo Burnett) also emphasised the individual treatment of clients: 'We feel we have to organise our management resources according to the specific needs of each client'. The extent of influence clients have over their agencies becomes more apparent after reading the following quotations. They are important in order to appreciate the weight clients carry in their agencies' eyes.

One of the agency executives cited a well-known hyperbole in the account: 'If the client's President has a cold, the agency gets pneumonia'. One executive from Y & R expressed his feelings as follows: 'I don't welcome nor tolerate any European co-ordination getting regularly involved in the business I am trying to pursue in the name of my client. I only take direction from the client'.

G. Phillips of DDB Needham for American Airlines said 'Some of the international accounts have accounted for setting up offices, especially for that company and grew from there'. One of McCann's co-ordinators admitted that 'Our______office was set up to service on an account-management basis for that specific client'.

The following quotation is valuable in that it accentuates the extent of matching between the client and the agency. Matching organisational charts was generally not sufficient for a satisfactory relationship. Agency and client philosophies of advertising style also needed to be in accord with each other to ensure a long-term smooth relationship. The following example clearly illustrates this:

> At the end of the commercial we had added a bit of film magic. That wonderful moment took two seconds out of the film. Logically it added nothing to the communication but it was the thing everybody remembered. The American client could not understand that. It was a bit European and creative, but they let us run it. It worked terribly well. By any objective standard, the advertising delivered, but imperceptibly we began to lose the account. I am sure because we were not their kind of people. At the end they moved to another agency.

Although not the basis of a specific question, one third of the account executives interviewed mentioned that they had lately had to reorganise their account on the agency side as the result of a similar transformation that had taken place within their client's structure, usually aligning their structure to fit that of their client's.

The following examples are the two most striking cases. They show the extent to which agencies will go to create structures corresponding to their clients. The first comes from one of BBDO's accounts. The client's budget had recently been increased from £3 million to £10 million. The client, therefore, was caught with a rather sparsely staffed marketing department for handling the entire marketing and sales-promotion activities. The account supervisor expressed the agency's problems:

> Inevitably, because there are only three key characters at the other end, you don't want to overstaff your agency either. Otherwise you have six agency people sitting there versus two of the client's for discussing every single minor detail. It does not work. You begin to outnumber them. Therefore we try to trim it down. We try to match and mirror their structure, but because they are understaffed it is extremely difficult.

The next example explains how the agency acquired its international network and how one particular client was the reason behind it. Practitioners usually emphasised close agency–client relationships in business with the help of anecdotes. The bonds formed, especially with account executives, would continue even after the executives changed agencies or formed their own practices. In some cases accounts would move with account executives – examples with happy endings. One such executive had come from Collett Dickenson Pearce. When he was there he handled a particular client's UK account. When he left to form his own practice, this account was one of his first clients. In 1983, the client's US management decided on a global marketing strategy and they appointed O & M as their global advertising agency. The account had to leave this executive's agency, which was a traumatic affair. The executive vowed at this point that he would never lose a client again for that reason, and that he would set up an international network. When his company bought the network and became international at the beginning of 1986, this same ex-client's UK management led a management buy-out to obtain the company from the USA and to make it a UK company. The occurrences were timed perfectly and the account was moved back to its first agency. They now handled it in seven European markets as well as in the USA.

The client's influence was, therefore, not simply constrained to reflecting its own organisational structure within its agencies: the client's weight can easily lead to far-reaching consequences in the agency. Agencies choose to remain understaffed so as not to outnumber their clients in meetings. Or they seek expansion on a worldwide basis, depending on the agency's perceptions of the client's weight and credit. If agencies do not come up to the expectations of their clients, the consequences for the agency, and, to a lesser extent, for the client, would be rather detrimental and damaging.

We will now look at the preparedness of clients to run global campaigns. This again stresses the client's power and role in the agency–client relationship. The agency executives who were interviewed mentioned that the client must be well organised and well prepared for global advertising before asking its agency to run a global campaign. If the client did not have line authority over its own affiliates to make them run the centrally produced campaign, then the agency could not ensure this for the client either. HQs and affiliates needed to agree beforehand between themselves. If there was conflict, then the 'agency could not pull some magic white rabbit out of a hat' to make those local markets accept the global campaign. Standardised campaigns worked well where HQs had line authority over the operating companies. This last issue raised another question: was it possible to run global campaigns only in highly centralised companies? The answer to that question will be found in Chapter 9. Having discussed agency–client relationships, HO involvement in agencies will be examined in the light of the points so far raised.

THE UNMENTIONABLE: AHO INVOLVEMENT

The accounts included in this book can be grouped, in general, according to the level of AHO involvement. The level of involvement was determined by the accounts' relationships with their clients, and can be classified as either 'high' or 'low'. Of the account executives interviewed, 60% stated that they had a high degree of HO involvement in the creation and production of the advertising used for their accounts. The accounts (22 out of the 37) with 'high' AHO involvement shared certain features. First, the agency's HO handled the account in the client's home country. The degree of involvement was, hence, high, at top-management levels both at the client and in the agency. If campaigns were created for the client's home country by the agency's HO, the same campaign would, most likely, be transferred to the agency's UK branch for use in the UK. Second, these accounts belonged to corporates that exercised a high degree of HQ involvement in the client's organisation. In other words, HQs had an influential role in their affiliates' marketing activities, including their advertising. Both characteristics showed that the client's structure was the determining factor in AHO involvement in individual accounts. If the client was more involved in their affiliates' advertising activities, then so was the AHO in their local offices. It is thus important to examine the general traits of clients who receive a high level of HQ involvement in order to understand similar accounts in agencies.

Clients that practised global marketing had certain features in common, even though these corporates used different expressions to sum up their corporate philosophy. These were described by account executives as 'think global, act local' or 'global marketing with local faces' or 'multilocal'. They all imply that strategic thinking and direction come from the centre. However, local affiliates' marketing and sales departments were granted flexibility to act in the manner they thought appropriate. The acceptance or otherwise of these centrally created campaigns was left to local management's discretion. The general manager of each local company was accountable and responsible for the business in that particular country, and if their authority was removed they could not be held responsible for that particular local operation. These top managers would also not shoulder the consequences of a decision that had been forced upon them. They would, additionally, lose effectiveness as a result of low morale, and would lose the co-operation of employees in those local markets. One executive expressed this as follows: 'They will have their fears reinforced about the loss of their own ability to influence events. They will be saying "we get this envelope through the post and that is apparently our advertising campaign"'.

When it came to running the advertising initiated by clients that received more HQ involvement, these clients basically believed in a central strategy: product groups were expected to have a central strategy that was protected by the aegis of a corporate strategy. However, local flexibility was permitted in the execution of this centralised strategy. Similarly, local managers were free to make up their minds to use the same or a different execution. This approach enabled affiliates to borrow good ideas from each other, the co-ordination function being borne by the HQs.

One of the world's leading soft-drinks manufacturers was quite centralised in producing and creating the advertising activities of its affiliates. A vast spender on advertising, its agency produced 15–20 TV commercials annually at HO. According to the needs of each local market, it let its affiliates choose to run whichever of these commercials they considered to be most appropriate for their own markets. Initiating contact with HO and asking for commercials were at the discretion of local offices: HO did not make any decisions for them. On the other hand, Guy Phillips (Account Executive of American Airlines at DDB) declared that the local client did not keep personnel for its UK advertising activities, which was strictly dealt with by HQ: 'Mainly because they are in 90 plus markets from America and abroad. They have to have one central department to organise it. Otherwise there will be anarchy'. This point raises the question of whether or not international companies need and, therefore, adopt, a more centralised style for practical reasons.

Having looked at 'high' AHO involvement accounts, we will now consider the trends that accounts with 'low' AHO involvement exhibit. A total of 40% of the interviewees (15 out of the 37) stated that they had relatively less involvement from their HOs while managing their accounts' UK advertising activities. When involvement was low it meant that the UK agency branch was more autonomous in developing the campaigns for that particular account. The agreement would usually be that, once the campaign was approved by the local client, the UK agency did not need to obtain the approval of its own AHO. This finding stresses the influential role clients played in their agencies. If the client relied more on its own affiliates, on its affiliates' good judgement, the client was, therefore, more decentralised in its approach, and its AHO (as well as the local agency offices that worked with the local client) would similarly reflect this autonomy.

When it came to running advertising campaigns for such accounts, the AHO would be informed of the development along general lines; they would be aware of the campaigns local agency offices were devising or running. However, the reporting system itself did not lead to tight control: a loose control system exhibited itself in the form of a quality control of the services given by the agency. The service given by the HO was not considered to be a replacement but an addition to local resources. This service was mainly in the form of co-ordinating information, materials and thinking from the rest of the world, and channelling good ideas to the appropriate areas, which included active local-office input to the agency's data-bank. Local offices were considered an asset to the agency's network; they were not considered to be mere branches that needed direction. Their contribution to the entire network was not denied, and they were relied upon, and expected, to take the initiative and to draw upon their creative resources for the benefit of the whole organisation.

Of all the accounts interviewed, the Shell account was the prototype of decentralisation. Caroline Marks, Senior Account Executive of Shell International at O & M, was originally interviewed in May 1988. However, consent to use the following quotations was granted by Peter Wilken, Account Director on the same account in October 1989, as Caroline Marks was no longer with O & M. Wilken refers to a quotation from Peter Holmes, Chairman of the Shell Transport and Trading Company, where he describes the Shell account: 'a highly decentralised organisation, which allows operating companies the optimum degree of autonomy and flexibility'. It was explained that this characteristic was, at one and the same time, Shell's strength and weakness. It was its strength because it was seen as a local, friendly and native company in every country it operated in: it had a local face in every market. Shell was acknowledged as an indigenous company, sensitive and reactive to local needs. It was its weakness because this characteristic permitted the 'not-invented-here' (NIH) syndrome to flourish: every agency in each market could hold up its hands at every new idea and claim that 'it's different here, because . . .' Wilken concludes that, without firm central direction, differences win over similarities. The final warning is directed to managers: potentially big ideas can be killed before birth because of the practical problems of managing them across borders.

It was, therefore, possible to encounter in corporates extreme cases of both decentralised and centralised approaches. Each and every one of them inevitably had its own advantages and disadvantages, but the crucial point seems to be to reach an optimum mix within the established framework of the corporate's culture.

When looking at these 'low' AHO involvement accounts, we again see certain similar characteristics. First, either they were not handled by the same AHO in the client's home country or that specific product/service was not marketed in the client's home country. However, both of these characteristics led to the same thing: if the AHO was not involved in the creation of the advertising campaign, the AHO would undertake a rather diminished role. Second, in these accounts, the agencies' London offices acted as regional (European) co-ordination – they directed the accounts' management totally from London. As is explained in Chapter 7, these regional offices were mostly at the same location as the agencies' UK branches, sometimes even in the same building although very much separate from each other.

If the account was handled entirely from London (in both creation and co-ordination aspects), this implied that the UK office was assigned the 'lead agency' on that account. The lead-agency concept is also examined in Chapter 7. However, whether international agencies had regional co-ordinations based in the UK, or the UK office was assigned the lead agency of that account, responsibility and authority were delegated to these separate units by their official HOs. In the cases where account executives mentioned 'low' HO involvement, they experienced this involvement from their European co-ordinators or they, as the UK office, were the European co-ordinators or the lead agency.

Before finishing this Chapter we need to look at the conditions that lead to increases in AHO involvement. Is it possible to avoid or, at least, to ease, AHO involvement? What prompts the AHO to jump into a local market and take over? Account executives admitted that HO involvement increased in their case if they, as the UK office, were faced with a crisis or a problem. One put it as 'when you do not return your profit, then the head office gets involved'. Yet another executive stated that their own HO and the client's HQ involvement increased when there was a lack of local marketing expertise in both the agency and the client. This lack of expertise could also be considered a 'problem'. Otherwise, 'if things are going well with the relationship, the senior management wants to "let sleeping dogs lie"'. Interestingly, the degree of involvement agencies had – whether high or low – was very much client driven. Clients set the style and tone of the relationship they were going to have. This was not only true of their own affiliates but also of their agencies and the agencies' worldwide network. The agencies adopted their clients' style in each account. If the client granted more autonomy to their local affiliates in their advertising decisions, AHOs also delegated more responsibility to the relevant offices working with the client's affiliates.

Considering all that has been mentioned here, we can say that in every account there is a 'big brother' watching over both agencies and clients. This is true for both decentralised and centralised clients. Big brother is the client's HQ. It is this big brother who decides to have a decentralised relationship with its own affiliates all around the globe, and this attitude is invariably inflicted on the AHO. The AHO, in return, adopts this decentralised approach and leaves its own local branches more or less on their own. Local agency branches will also have more say in the advertising that will be run for that particular international client's local affiliate.

If, on the other hand, the client's HQ is a very centralised body, then this highly centralised structure will be reflected in all the parties involved. Local affiliates will become highly dependent on their HQs. The AHO will probably end up creating the prototype campaign for the client's HQ. Local agency branches will possibly run campaigns they receive in the post from their own HOs. And we know the rest ... With every type of client it is, therefore, important to be aware of the fact that the international client's HQ is 'big brother': he is watching you wherever you are and whatever you do. He most definitely sets the tone of the relationship in all parties involved – in both the client's and the agency's organisational structures. A simple version of this organisational structure is illustrated in Figure 6.1. We examine in the next chapter whether or not the organisational charts adopted by international clients and agencies are more complicated than that described earlier. We will also meet the 'black sheep' of agencies. Weren't we talking about the black sheep of agencies in this chapter? The answer to this question is 'no'. We cannot talk about good agency–client relationships if clients are considered to be the black sheep of agencies – as agency customers, clients can only be kings. We have not met the agency black sheep yet, but introducing them is inevitable in the next chapter.

7
INTERNATIONAL ADVERTISING AGENCIES – TWO-HEADED DRAGONS

Our study revealed another surprising fact about international advertising agencies: these agencies had two head offices (HOs), one actual and one official.

OFFICIAL HOs AND ACTUAL HOs (OR 'LEAD AGENCIES')

Official HOs are where holding companies are based and registered. Six of the agencies contacted were based in New York, two in Chicago and five in London. These were the official HOs. However, a separate office was also involved in the account's advertising – in its creation and production. This was the nearest agency branch to the client's HQ. This rule of thumb was obviously only true for international clients. Table 7.1 lists the location of those agency HOs and client HQs whose accounts were interviewed when conducting the study.

Of the accounts interviewed, 84% (26 out of the 31) had a separate actual HO apart from their official HOs. These actual HOs were in the same town, if not in the same building, as the client's HQ. Actual and official HOs were in the same town in 11 accounts out of the 31 (35%). Of these 11 accounts, 9 had official HOs in the same city as the clients' HQs. In other words, the nearest agency to the client happened also to be the official HO. In these 9 accounts, the official and actual HO roles were undertaken by the same agency branch. The two exceptions to this were Gillette and American Airlines. Gillette had recently formed North Atlantic Region within BBDO's New York office. However, the client was based in Boston. Before the North Atlantic Region was set up, BBDO (London) handled European co-ordination because Regional European Gillette was based in Isleworth. BBDO and the London and New York offices now had close contact even in the daily ins and outs of campaigns.

As for American Airlines, the UK office created the pan-European advertising. DDB Needham (New York) was in close contact with their London office because the client wanted an agency link in the USA. American Airlines had also been based in New York until eight years ago, when they moved to Dallas because of the nature of their operations. In the airline business, Dallas is one of the major middle destinations used in coast-to-coast domestic flights. These two accounts, therefore, had specific reasons for their different structures.

There were three accounts where the agency's actual HO did not match the client's HQ. These were Martini and Unilever's Edible Fats and Frozen Foods. Martini was a very centralised account: only two men led decisions on their worldwide advertising (see Chapter 9). The agency did not, therefore, have to be in the client's vicinity. There was no need for coaxing to sell campaign ideas to different offices. The agency in the two exceptions from Unilever had their International Co-ordination Units within McCann's London office. The company's International Co-ordinators were based in Rotterdam. Being an Anglo-Dutch company, the co-ordination functions for their different product groups were (probably) split between the Rotterdam and London operations.

When it came to choosing actual HOs, agencies generally selected these according to where their client was based. If the client had a European co-ordination unit, the agency would also set up a similar unit, close to the client's. The executives in these offices had equal levels of authority and responsibility: each client executive had a shadow in the agency.

G. Phillips of DDB summarised this as follows: 'When you get to international clients, then the office which is in that client's country or nearest to the client takes the position of a lead country for that specific account. For example, our German office was set up for the Volkswagen account'.

Another striking example elaborates the same point:

> The way we operate on the account is that the lead agency is in Chicago, where the client's headquarter is. They had the account for decades. They know the business and the people well. They are very, very close. It is good to plug in our Chicago office's expertise. They know what the client is thinking at senior level.

If all advertising is handled by the actual HOs of international agencies that are closest to the clients' HQs, what is the point of having official HOs? Have they any other function in international accounts, other than adding another layer to management and increasing the dead wood?

Local agencies had a relationship with their official HOs, but this was a formal one. It was conducted at senior management levels by both the client and the agency. The official HO knew the specific accounts and the clients included in the agency's portfolio. They were aware of these accounts as large sections of business but did not become involved in advertising campaign developments for their international clients. The official HOs had, in the main, administrative links with their local agencies. Local agencies reported their profitability and end-of-year figures on these international accounts. Official HOs were the registered offices; they sent their annual reports to the local

Table 7.1 Actual and official HOs of the international accounts and the international clients' HQs

Agencies and accounts	Official HOs	Actual HOs	International clients' base
BBDO	NY		
Account A		NY	NY
Apple		LA (Lead Agency) Eu. France	Cupertino (USA)/ Eu. France
Account B		Chicago (Lead Agency)	Chicago
Gillette*		NY	Boston/Eu. Co-or., Isleworth
DDB Needham	NY		
American Air[†]		NY. Eu. London	Dallas
Agency Z	London		
Account C		Lead Agency close to the client	
Foote Cone & Belding	Chicago		
C. Palmolive soap		Eu. Co-or. London	Eu. Co-or. London
Harrison Int.	NY		
Braun		London	UK client
Lilt		London	Atlanta and UK
Fanta		Atlanta	Atlanta and UK
J. Walter Thompson	London		
Account K		Int. Div. London	UK
Account M		Int. Div. London	UK
Agency Y	London		
Account D		WW Co-or. London	Int. Div. New Haven, UK
McCann-Erickson	NY		
Account L		Atlanta	Atlanta
Unilever Edible Fats[‡]		WW Co-or. London	WW Co-or. Rotterdam
Unilever Frozen Foods[‡]		Eu. Co-or. London	Eu. Co-or. Rotterdam
Martini §		London (Lead Agency)	Turin, Italy
Esso		Int. Co-or. NY/Exxon (Houston)	Int. Co-or. NJ/ Exxon (Houston)
Ogilvy & Mather	NY		
Philips Cons. Elec.		Eu. Co-or. Holland	WW Co-or. Holland
American Express		WW Co-or. NY	WW Co-or. NY
Ford		Eu. Management Supervision UK	Ford of Eu. Essex
Shell Int.		Int. Co-or. London	Int. Co-or. London

Table 7.1 Continued.

Agencies and accounts	Official HOs	Actual HOs	International clients' base
Agency X	London		
Account E		WW Co-or. London	WW. Co-or. London
Agency W	London		
Account F		NY/Eu. Co-or. London	NY/Eu. Co-or. London
Account G		Sister Agency Eu. Co-or. London	NY/Eu. HQs London
Young & Rubicam	NY		
TWA		Eu. Co-or. London	Int. HQs Knightsbridge
Account H		Int. Co-or. NY	Business Development Group NY
Account I		London (Lead Agency)	HQs London
Account J		Eu. Co-or. London	Int. HQs nr. London
Kodak batteries		Eu. Co-or. London	Eu. Co-or. London
Air Canada		Eu. Co-or. London	Int. Advertising London

Abbreviations
Eu. – Europe; Int. – International; Co-or. – Co-ordination; Div. – Division; WW – Worldwide; NY – New York; NJ – New Jersey; LA – Los Angeles.

Notes
* A recent change took place. European Co-ordination was moved from London to New York and grouped under North Atlantic Region.
† American Airlines moved to Dallas eight years ago. Before that they were also in New York.
‡ Exceptional cases.
§ Very centralised client.

agencies as their holding companies. The reporting system generally consisted of financial issues, not the development of specific advertising campaigns. Campaign development was the actual HO's responsibility. Local agencies did not usually have direct contact with the official HOs, but they communicated closely with their actual HOs for creative guidance and direction.

R. Steward of McCann's illustrated this point as 'McCann (New York) is interested in such a large piece of business. But there is no organisation function in New York, set up purely for Unilever'. P. Nelson, also from McCann's, expressed how this worked in his accounts:

> McCann's works on looking after clients in the best geographical location. We would get New York involved in financial decisions. If the client wants to negotiate commission or profitability, then they get involved. However, in terms of actually producing the advertising strategy or the advertising executions, that is handled from London.

One other executive of Ogilvy & Mather (O & M) said that 'Our head office, being in New York, has effectively no involvement. They say they cannot make European decisions. We get very frequent reviews, but no day-to-day participation'.

At the start of the study we had intended to examine international agencies with non-UK parents. We wanted to contact these international agencies' London offices to try to capture the involvement they had from their HOs when developing international campaigns. However, 5 of the 13 agencies interviewed had UK parents at the time of the interviews. The information gathered from these agencies is still included in the book because we were not interested in agency ownerships.

Our early results showed that agencies had two HOs (official and actual), and that these were two separate entities. Our main interest, though, lay with actual HOs as these were the ones who became involved in international campaigns. As long as the agencies we contacted had actual HOs outside the UK they could be included. Hence the sample also contained these 5 UK-based agencies.

The main factor in determining the direction of campaign transfers was the client's location. Accordingly, the local agency branch nearest to the client would be involved in campaign development. This agency would undertake the actual HO role. It would then transfer the same international campaign to its sister agencies (other local branches) who happened to have the same international account in their portfolios. The key element of this book was not where agencies were registered but a study of the various international campaigns created outside the UK and then transferred to the UK.

As was also shown in Chapter 6, this chapter has emphasised how, in international accounts, agency behaviour is very much client-led: international clients determined the agency's actual HO for that particular account. These actual HOs sometimes acted as a 'lead agency'. In other accounts they would have European co-ordination or international co-ordination – it all depended on the client's structure and needs. However they were set up, these actual HOs were involved in campaign development and in its transfer across countries. Campaign development by lead agencies is examined in Chapter 9.

Lead Agencies and Clients

Assigning a 'lead agency' a specific account had deep-rooted implications. One of the executives interviewed (who wished to remain anonymous) explained this as follows:

> For US clients there needs to be a strong US office. Ownership is different. Which office clients accept as the head office is very important. It is mainly nationalistic feelings coming across. It is even emotionally difficult for a US client to employ a UK-based agency.

This executive was in an agency that had historically been a US agency (with a New York HO), until they had been acquired by a UK agency.

J. Walter Thompson's (JWT) buy-out by UK-based WPP had a similar effect on JWT's relationships with its clients. An executive outside JWT pointed out that JWT's relationship with some of its US-based clients had soared after its ownership had changed hands. It was also added that some clients even moved to other agencies as a result of this change in ownership. JWT still considered itself as a US-based agency even though it was now owned by WPP. The US office was still actively involved in the creative side of advertising. WPP encouraged this. Also, WPP (who did not have any other agency under its corporate umbrella) wanted JWT to hold on to its own identity (1).

Another executive put his observations as follows: 'As with any nationality, there is some resistance to dealing with an agency with head office in another country, another culture. There is some feeling amongst clients' senior management levels that operationally on a day-to-day basis things might get done faster if both organisations are in the same country'.

These quotations demonstrate that there were, most probably, nationalistic reasons for assigning the closest agency as the lead agency for the client's HQ. The practical reasons for having a lead agency cannot be denied, and these include proximity, quicker response, easier communication and more frequent contact. However, having a lead agency definitely helped the client to overcome the feelings of dealing with foreigners. Clients felt safer, more secure and, most of all, at ease with their lead agencies, mainly because they felt they were sharing the same language and the same business environment with them.

It is now time to turn our attention to agency regional European HOs: do different patterns emerge in these units' structures in the various international accounts? Regional HOs are sometimes considered to be European lead agencies, but only when their clients have formed similar international co-ordinations for Europe.

REGIONAL EUROPEAN HOs – THE BLACK SHEEP OF AGENCIES?

The formation by agencies of regional HOs for Europe depended on the individual accounts. If their clients had one, then the agencies would also establish a regional HO on that account. Within the same agency you sometimes see a regional HO and sometimes you do not, depending on accounts and clients.

Only Leo Burnett (of the 13 agencies examined) had a permanent regional division, irrespective of whether or not their individual clients had one. This regional division was integrated into Leo Burnett's own organisational structure. Each region was headed by a regional managing director. Inter-agency co-ordination was the main function of these international divisions: they acted as a control entity, setting goals and monitoring progress with a centralised creative ability.

The next example is rather surprising, and it clearly illustrates the client's influence. The client had divided Europe into five areas: Northern, South Western, Central and Eastern Europe (the fifth consisted solely of Italy!). This client's agency had also split itself in a similar way – Italy being treated as a separate group by itself. The client did not have regional HQs in Europe, and nor did the agency.

Another executive summed up the reasons for having regional HOs as 'Agencies need to be strong in New York and in London'. London offices were usually chosen as regional HOs because London is a central location between the USA and Europe. The UK is also close to other major European markets, and British expertise in advertising is considered a major factor in this decision.

Another reason why agency executives replicate their client's organisations in minute detail was given by an account director at O & M: 'It is mainly working effectiveness, but being a service industry turns it into a "must"'. The client has divided Europe into two regions, Northern and Southern. If the agency had divided Europe into Scandinavia, Central Europe and Mediterranean countries, responsibilities would clash. This could cause complications: Who would go to which meetings? Who would be whose counterpart? Who would communicate with whom? Hence there were major practical reasons for setting up a similar organisation to that of clients.

Perhaps a less rational reason was to show goodwill and courtesy to the client by matching their set-up. Less rational though this may be, it definitely helped in the smooth conduct of business between partners. This exhibition of goodwill by agencies was more impressive than it appeared to the naked eye: one had to examine local agencies' feelings towards their regional HOs in order to appreciate what these agencies were sacrificing for their clients.

There was a definitely psychic distance between local agencies and their regional co-ordination units; but local clients did not seem to consider their own regional HQs as their closest buddies either. The following anonymous quotations help to elaborate these points with their lively use of metaphor:

> The UK client and their Regional Headquarters are a floor apart, but don't share decisions. At the agency side, we are trying to develop links between our UK offices and the European Co-ordination.

> There is even a physical split. If you take the right-hand side of the corridor, down there, that is European International. Carpets are deeper, desks are bigger.

> The organisation is further complicated, although we would like to think strengthened, by the fact that outside our client's domestic market, there is also a Central International Headquarters, as well as European Headquarters.

> Our relationship with our International Co-ordination is one of distrust and dislike! Partly because by the sheer nature that they are international people, dealing with international clients, they start thinking and acting like clients. We send our scripts to them. They add their own interpretations and eventually sell the work not in the way it was intended to initially. We do not like their involvement and see them as interfering and going behind our backs, also affecting what could be a good client–agency relationship if it were allowed to develop.

> We call them 'international seagulls'. They arrive in a country, eat their food, drink their drinks and leave the country after messing up their shores. They like interfering, as it is the only justification of their job.

> They start acting as advertisers. Our job is to protect the consumer and to be honest. Not to say what the client wants to hear. They become rather like second clients.

Taking an optimistic view, these feelings could not be labelled as hostile. However they exhibit agencies' sheer determination to keep their regional HOs at arm's length – if only they could. If they did not show resentment they certainly had reservations. Regional HOs were blamed for different things – from tabulatory gigantism (obsession with large-size desks) to being world-renown polluters. Could they be called anything else but the black sheep of international advertising agencies?

It must also be said that account executives gave credit to their international co-ordination units where credit was due. They were often cited as being vast data-banks. They were also good at keeping track of market information compiled from all round the globe. Some of the international co-ordinators whom we talked to did not, themselves, see their roles as all that prominent or far-reaching. One said that 'In a sense, we act as a "glorified post box". Work comes in from South East Asia and we think it might be useful in South America. We then copy it and pass it on'. Strangely enough, smaller and larger local agencies reacted differently towards their international co-ordination unit's advice. The executives interviewed all agreed that smaller branches (such as Portugal, Greece and Turkey) were much more appreciative of the help they received from these units. In these countries production quality was considered to be lower than the European norm. They would ask for advice and, in return, they would be grateful for the support they received. On the other hand, 'Bigger offices have the same number of problems but they would not want advice, because they have got more resources, more experience, more sophistication in marketing. They feel they do not need anyone else getting involved. However, they do not see things in an international perspective'.

Account executives generally named the French and UK offices as the two most difficult to persuade to use material sent from the centre:

> France will as usual almost certainly go its own way! It is a particular problem which a lot of companies have. Integrating France into this international process, unless the client is very strong and demands it, is very hard! UK and France are two difficult markets to integrate, the most individualistic, probably the most nationalistic and chauvinistic!

Once again the client's influential role was apparent. The same split was also confirmed in the client. Smaller local clients did not mind the help they received from their co-ordination units:

> The smaller ones are perfectly happy to go along with the centre's view, because the amount of resources they can put behind the process of advertising is very limited! If they can get a lot of help and support and perhaps even materials from the centre, they feel they can use the money they have locally more effectively, perhaps by putting it into media expenditure rather than into production.

However, larger clients were worried about losing their independence and authority. They were concerned about losing their ability to change agencies: 'Whether they want to do that or not is immaterial. The fact that they cannot, is what is important and they resent that'.

This chapter has also shown the power and weight clients have over their agencies. Agencies had regional HOs if their clients had a similar set-up. UK agencies, besides, also felt betrayed by their regional HOs. They felt they were receiving more interference than they would have liked. What is more, the reaction of smaller and larger local agencies towards their regional HOs varied considerably. Smaller local agencies welcomed the co-ordination unit's help or even intervention; larger agencies totally rejected it. The UK agencies' negative reactions towards regional HOs' advice were a further confirmation of their size: it seems that these regional HOs could do with a bit of Peter's Placebo. Placebo states that 'An ounce of image is worth a pound of performance'(2). These regional HOs definitely suffered a lack of image in the eyes of their London branches! Overall, clients and agencies were true replicas of each other. They resembled each other in every respect. They even shared the same provisos towards their regional HOs/HQs!

THE 'MIRRORING EFFECT': ORGANISATIONAL STRUCTURE IN GLOBAL CAMPAIGNS

Before conducting the interviews with agency executives four parties seemed to be involved in the creation of an international advertising campaign (a simplified version of this is given in Chapter 6, Figure 6.1). These four parties were the agency HO, the client's HQ, the local agency branch and the local client (affiliate company).

However, the observations made about international advertising agencies (discussed in this and the previous chapter) enable us to see the more detailed organisational structure adopted while running global campaigns. Figure 7.1 shows the more comprehensive structure found in international agencies and in multinational clients. Once again the starting point is the client: to supply the best service and to satisfy the clients, agencies mirrored their clients' organisational structures (the 'mirroring effect'). This matching was carried out to such an extent that, if clients had a regional European co-ordination unit, then agencies would form one as well and, as has already been mentioned, the UK agency and the co-ordinating body could even be within the same agency and building (though operating separately).

Links with the Lead Agency

The nearest agency branch to the client's HQ would be assigned the lead agency on that particular account (this obviously did not always coincide with where the agency's official HO was based). These lead agencies handled the

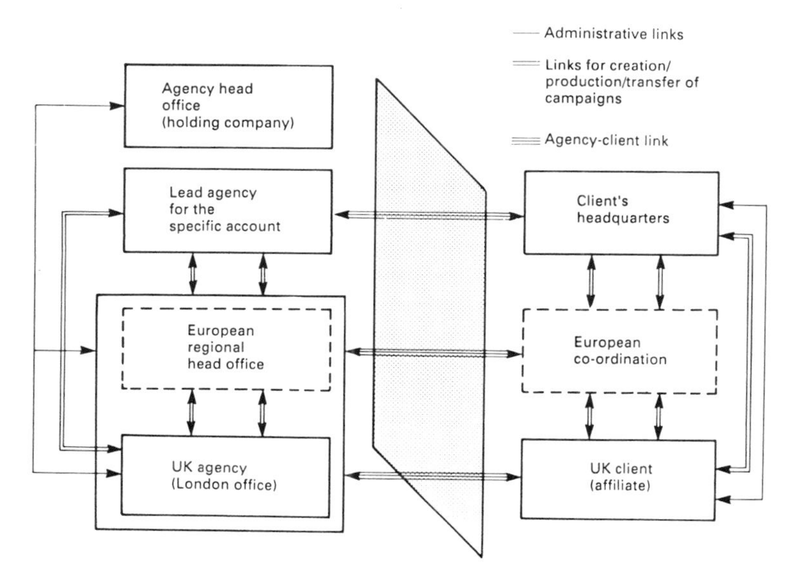

Figure 7.1 How agencies and clients organise themselves when conducting global advertising campaigns (the 'mirroring effect')

creation of international campaigns. They developed it from an idea, and possibly produced it or co-ordinated its production. Following its production, they transferred the campaign to other local agencies that had the same account. Throughout the campaign's preparations there was constant contact among the lead agency, the European regional HO and the UK office. Furthermore, the lead agency had a very kaleidoscopic nature, as it changed from one account to another: the lead agency for account X might be transformed into an ordinary local agency for account Y, where client Y is based in a different country or town.

Links with the Official HO

Yet another component in developing global campaigns was the agency's official HO (the agency's holding company). The official HO had administrative links with the European HO, as well as with individual agency branches. Local agency branches reported to their holding company on financial issues, such as meeting their annual targets. Official HOs did not interfere in creating advertising to run in local markets – campaign development was the lead agency's responsibility. However, they did have the authority that goes with responsibility. In very rare cases official HOs did become involved in campaign developments if the client's HQ and the agency's official HO happened to be based in the same city. Lead agency and the official HO responsibilities then overlapped.

Nothing has been mentioned here about the links between the official HO and the lead agency. That relationship falls outside the scope of this book. However, one important thing can be said about it: the two roles were always segregated within the agencies contacted.

The Agency–Client Link

The agency–client link was the third link observed. Again, agencies structured themselves to match their clients. Each office kept in contact with its corresponding office. For example, the UK agency would never contact directly the client's HQ. Should such a need arise, they would involve the lead agency or the UK agency would take the problem to the UK client so that the client could handle it within its own organisation.

Links within the Client's Organisation

Finally, the links observed within the client resembled the links witnessed in the agency, though with minor modifications. Three parties (client's HQ, European co-ordination and UK affiliate) each had administrative links and links for campaign development with each other. The client was not involved in the creation of the campaign (although, of course the client had initiated it). They knew their products and knew (or were supposed to know) what was needed for their brand, but lacked the skills required to create it. Therefore within the client's organisation ideas were exchanged regarding a brief, product policy, and all other relevant marketing-mix elements.

'TRUST YOUR AGENCY': A TALE THAT CAME TRUE

To end this chapter on an optimistic note, we have included the famous Avis campaign, as R. Townsend has described it (3). Townsend was the President of Avis and he sums up the moral of his entire experience there as 'Don't hire a master to paint you a masterpiece and then assign a roomful of schoolboy-artists to look over his shoulder and suggest improvements'. This reminds one of Ogilvy's 'Committees can criticise but can't create' (4).

The story of the Avis campaign is as follows. After firing its old agency, the company was looking for a new one that would give a simple answer to its knotty question: 'How do we get five million dollars of advertising for one million dollars?' (Five million was their competitor's advertising budget.) Finally, Bill Bernbach of DDB came up with an answer. He said (3, pp. 17–18)

> If you want five times the impact, give us ninety days to learn enough about your business to apply our skills and then run every ad we write where we tell you to run it. If you run them just as we write them, you'll have every art director and copy writer in my shop moonlighting on your account.

1. Avis will never know as much about advertising as DDB and DDB will never know as much about the rent-a-car business as Avis.
2. The purpose of the advertising is to persuade the frequent business renter (whether on a business trip, a vacation trip or renting an extra car at home) to try Avis.
3. A serious attempt will be made to create advertising with five times the effectiveness (see No. 2 above) of the competition's advertising.
4. To this end, Avis will approve or disapprove, not try to improve, ads which are submitted. Any changes suggested by Avis must be grounded on a material operating defect (a wrong uniform for example).
5. To this end, DDB will only submit for approval those ads which they as an Agency recommend. They will not 'see what Avis thinks of that one'.
6. Media selection should be the primary responsibility of DDB. However, DDB is expected to take the initiative to get guidance from Avis in weighting of markets or special situations, particularly in those areas where cold numbers do not indicate the real picture. Media judgements are open to discussion. The conviction would prevail. Compromises should be avoided.

Figure 7.2 Avis Rent-a-Car's advertising philosophy (Reference 3, p. 19)

Avis and DDB agreed, framed their advertising philosophy and hung it up on everybody's wall both at the client's and at the agency. It read as in Figure 7.2.

When Bill Bernbach came back at the end of ninety days, he said he was sorry but he could only say that Avis was the second largest rent-a-car company and that its employees were trying harder. He added that he didn't like the ads very much, but this was all they had managed to come up with. Although the Avis people were not excited about the ads either, they ran them as DDB had recommended, in line with their advertising philosophy. Townsend concludes by saying 'The rest is history. Our internal sales growth rate increased from 10% to 35% in the next couple of years'.

It is totally unknown whether or not Avis and DDB were devoted followers of the 'mirroring effect'. However, the story delivers a strong message: the agency and the client were able to communicate with each other. They kept communication lines open at all times. They also made sure that they opened their hearts to each other. Neither side seems to have compromised its honesty, even under the gloomiest and most dismal conditions. (Could anything be more dreary for an agency than to say 'We don't like the campaign we have produced, but we haven't got anything else, either?'). I believe their other strong point was their respect of specialisation. Is anything more simple than saying, 'agencies know agency business best. Car-rental people know the car-rental business best'? This sounds simple almost to the point of being primitive, but it is the language of common sense. One cannot help but feel a little anger, a little jealousy: why cannot such sound agency–client relationships become the norm rather than the exception?

REFERENCES

1. What does WPP stand for? (1988) *The Sunday Times*, 19 June, p. D5.
2. Peter, L. and Hull, J. R. (1970) *The Peter Principle*, Pan Books, London.
3. Townsend, R. (1983) *Up the Organisation*, Hodder & Stoughton, Sevenoaks.
4. Ogilvy, D. (1983) *Ogilvy on Advertising*, Pan Books, London.

8

MAKING THE GOOD BETTER: ACCOUNT EXECUTIVES AND GLOBAL CAMPAIGNS

Of the account executives interviewed, 57% reported problems when transferring campaigns across countries. They concluded that the difficulties generally outweighed the gains made. Table 8.1 summarises account executives' feelings.

Alternatively, 27% were 'totally for it' and 17% said that it 'does not cause problems', giving a total of 44% of positive attitudes. These account executives were, interestingly, either international co-ordinators or pan-European co-ordinators. Additionally, in those accounts where campaign transfers took place frequently (possibly on a regular basis), the account executives showed a more favourable inclination towards global advertising (account executives exhibiting negative attitudes did not experience many transfers). The opponents of global advertising had had, in the past, major problems when trying to use transfers in the UK, hence regarding global advertising as being very difficult to implement. None of the account executives interviewed declined to express an opinion on global advertising.

Account executives belonging to the same agencies expressed similar views to each other: executives in BBDO and J. Walter Thompson (JWT) were more enthusiastic about global advertising, while Ogilvy & Mather (O & M), Young & Rubicam (Y & R), McCann's and Harrison Interpublic executives challenged it.

Table 8.1 Account executives' feelings towards transferring global campaigns

Feelings towards transfers	Frequency	%
'Totally for it'	8	26.7
'Does not cause problems'	5	16.7
'No idea'	—	—
'Very hard to implement'	14	46.7
'Totally against it'	3	10.0
Total	30	100.0

THE ONGOING TUG OF WAR: HEADS VERSUS HEARTS

Account executives supportive of global advertising gave wide-ranging reasons to back up their views: economies of scale, increase in world travel, the world becoming a smaller place through travel, and better and quicker communication facilities, etc. A global campaign helped to prevent dissonances in brand cultures from one country to another.

D. Delane (Gillette Account Supervisor at BBDO) said that 'Global advertising does not need to be the lowest common denominator. It is that way if you make it that way. It is more difficult, but if you do your homework properly and if you have a very clear, correct strategy, it can be impactful'. F. Clementis of Foote Cone & Belding (FCB) emphasised a further aspect: 'Coming up with good ideas is so rare. Once struck, it should be exploited fully'.

Other reasons were also given. For example, the reasoning was slightly different for cola products (not individual brands but the coloured fizzy-drinks market). One executive expressed this reasoning as follows: '[The] Cola market has all its heritage in the US. It is selling cola with American imagery and heritage. Because people see cola as an American product. Because there is no language difference between the US and the UK'. Commercials for these products, wherever they were produced, were given an intentional American look, with an American setting, cast and accent. They had to look American in order to be able to sell, because cola was an American product.

Three executives mentioned the use of a general theme with a local execution, the most commonly used phrase being 'Think global, act local'. One executive said it was important to identify the core elements in an ad, and that these elements needed to be understood fully first before transferring it to another country. He suggested retaining the core elements while making adaptations to the ad's 'supportive elements' in local markets. Although these arguments seem sound, a different execution for each country would actually cancel out the major advantage of 'globalism' – cost savings. We will now turn to the prerequisites for running global ads.

N. Thurlow of BBDO on the Apple Computer account explained that the product first needed to have a global marketing perspective. In other words, a synergy of product and consumer needs was necessary. Another executive indicated that global advertising is more suitable for young target groups and for fun products. P. Axten emphasised that, in the youth market, homogeneous youth products were more suitable. He also mentioned the trends and fashions of the day, such as 'healthier eating'.

One executive referred to three exceptional markets where global campaigns could not be run: the Middle East, Japan and the USA. In Japan and the Middle East, the visuals used in ads that were based heavily on Western culture would not have an impact. The reasons for excluding the USA, on the other hand, were different. Over the years, US management has traded higher margins with high volume, therefore offering large discounts and making the product a cheap one. To upmarket a product in the USA requires a different campaign. This is a good example of enhancing the role of consistent product positioning across borders to ensure the success of the campaign (the same point was also made by opponents of global advertising). The executive who raised the issue of exceptions also identified products that had globalisation engraved on them: in the main, status symbol brands used by status conscious consumers who were cosmopolitan but not necessarily young. Brands with a designer's name were an extension of their self-image, and globalisation was required to sustain their current positioning.

When looking at problems, there was only one supporter who acknowledged difficulties and he referred to its legal aspects. For example, in Malaysia, in order to be able to show a film on TV, it had to be shot locally. In addition, in countries comprising different ethnic groups, legislation forced an ethnic balance in commercials. He had faced problems in Malaysia with a commercial for a shampoo. To retain ethnic balance they used a Malaysian hairdresser and a Euro-Asian model. However, they were confronted by a religious commandment: the Moslem Malaysian hairdresser would not touch the model's hair. In the end, the hairdresser recommended the shampoo without touching the model's hair or her head. The advertisement, however, did not work.

This same executive also emphasised the financial problems in countries such as Greece, India and Brazil, where the transfer of foreign currency was either very difficult or completely illegal. These countries, therefore, could not share the costs of central production, and this prohibited them from making any contribution. Interestingly, this was a point raised as a hindrance to global campaigns, rather than a problem faced as a result of practising global campaigns!

The account executives interviewed generally had reservations about global advertising – they were more questioning and agreed that a successful global ad was the exception rather than the rule. The opponents of global advertising expressed their views in a similar fashion:

> For the majority of brands you can get better ads locally. In an ideal world the strategy should be uniform in each country. Unless you can secure that, most international advertising is weak. It is a compromise.
>
> You end up with a lowest common denominator, so that it works everywhere. It usually ends up being a wallpaper, so that nobody remembers it in any country.

Account executives also had interesting comments to make on cost savings. A. Gledhill of TWA put it as follows:

> In global advertising, you have to ignore every sort of regional variance. Then you nullify the financial advantages you have had. Because in each country you will be 5%, 10% or 15% off target. When you add these percentages up, then maybe you have undone the good in the first place.

An account manager at Y & R said that 'Yes, it has its economies of scale, but I am not entirely sure whether that could not also be a false con'. R. Rippin, an International Account Director at O & M, expressed his views as follows:

As long as you don't lose too much local effectiveness, then gains can be made. However, there is a caveat. In the first period it is quite likely that real costs will actually go up. Not only in the adaptation side, but the whole process would need a lot more consultation which is added into costs. It involves quite a number of senior people, with the client's organisation being involved in a series of discussions. You also need to spend a lot of time thinking about the issue. Then selling it throughout the organisation... That can go on quite easily for years, because it is a very tortuous process. It requires very strong selling unless you have a highly autocratic client, one-man-band. In a more typical Western company, there is a high degree of consensus required. There are people who disagree all the time. Therefore, it requires a lot of selling that takes a lot of time. Although it most certainly will not be publicised.

It will require the use of reserves. If we are going to make a saving of 20 and if we are 100 now, it might be 80 in ten years. But we should realise it can be 120 for the first five years, which is a bit shattering to people who sometimes write down lists of criteria for why global ads are a good idea. You often see the list that has right at the top, number one 'cost savings'. That is an absolute blow. The start-up costs are much more than initially predicted when you sit down to think about it.

An account director from O & M explained his objections thus:

Only seeing Europe tells you that the globe is not homogeneous. Italians and British absolutely don't have anything in common. Ford is an interesting case, because they sell the same cars everywhere. In Spain we are considered young and dynamic. In France, boring. In Italy, simply a car for people who cannot afford Fiats! They compete in the discount market. Whereas in Britain you only buy a Fiat if you can't afford a Ford.

Secondly, they break down by income, by size. In Italy, 80% of the market is B class – Fiesta, Peugeot, Fiat Uno, small compact cars. In Norway, that is 11% of the market. Norwegians want bigger cars. That is just the car market, where everyone is selling completely identical products. There are no branding problems or product differences, but total variation in markets, imagery of mark. How can you run similar campaigns?

Yet another executive similarly challenged global advertising and agencies: 'More sophisticated global marketing will be the one that pays more attention to local differences. Global brands are desirable, but insensitive too'. If global advertising is something to be avoided to be safe, should it be avoided at all times? Or are there certain conditions that need to be fulfilled first? The opponents of global advertising referred to slightly different prerequisites than its supporters. The most cited ones were as follows:

- It depends on the product and brand property.
- It is easier for homogeneous brands that have the same product positioning and that share the same stage of product life-cycle (PLC) in their countries of origin and in the other countries they will be transferred to.
- It needs to have a universal message, probably with an emotional promise.

T. Symington of Harrisons (Account Director for Braun) gave an interesting example of why brands need to be in the same or similar stages of PLC before planning any campaign transfers:

Food processors are very new in Canada. You have to tell consumers what it does, how it works. Therefore we couldn't use the UK commercial. However, we used the same setting, but shot two different films. They were both written up around the same set-ups, but actual messages, communication strategies were different.

R. Steward of McCann's underlined the client's role and how crucial it was in providing the necessary infrastructure before any steps were taken for transfers: 'Each company should be good in ground presence in each country and control each company in some way, either by persuasion, coercion or dictation. If not, then each affiliate would do their own thing'. Not surprisingly, more problems were mentioned by the opponents of global advertising, and these problems were the intricate, complex and involved aspects of management. Opponents stressed the discrepancies in the degrees of sophistication reached by different countries in advertising. They regarded the pan-European approach to be more acceptable than globalism.

A. Shingleton of McCann's on the Martini account expressed this as follows: 'Some markets are more mature in terms of advertising. A campaign which is right for the UK may not be right for Latin America for 2–3 years to come. Then you take the middle course to run it everywhere'.

Differences in advertising legislation in countries were also mentioned. A. Shingleton gave examples about alcohol: 'In France you can't have any alcohol advertising on TV. In the press, you can have the bottle and a glass. In South America you can have almost anything'.

Other legal prohibitions were as follows:

You can't show children all by themselves in France. They should always be accompanied by families.

In France, they just started allowing airline commercials on TV.

In Germany and Switzerland you can refer to competitors' products as 'normal batteries' but not in the UK. Ideally we wanted to show the whole range of batteries. We did that in Switzerland, but not in the UK and Germany. In the script we were saying 'Lithium lasts twice as much'. By showing all three batteries, it was considered that we were misleading consumers.

In Germany you have to clear your copy with an organisation. Even then, a competitor can complain without identifying itself. Then you are pulled off the air until you prove you are not guilty. In the UK it is just the opposite. If there is a complaint, you are allowed to stay on air until you are proven guilty. Here the motto is 'innocent until proven guilty'.

The last point relates to the Federal Republic of Germany's 1909 Act that prohibits unfair competition (amended in 1965 and 1969, and originally called *Gesetz gegen den unlauteren Wettbewerb*). Rijkens and Miracle (1, p. 299) point out that, in Germany, Article 3 (of the Council of Ministers, spring 1984 directive) aims to stop misleading advertising being used as an instrument of competition in business. They also stated that in Germany and Italy an injunction may be requested without proof of fault or intention on the part of the defendant (*ibid*. p. 287). On the other hand, the UK Trade Descriptions Act (1968, amended 1972) bans the false descriptions of goods, false or misleading information about products or false statements about certain services, and this is a ban enforced through criminal law. Therefore, although member states had until September 1986 to bring their national laws into conformity with the

Council of Ministers' September 1984 directive on misleading advertising (*ibid.* p. 121), the batteries example shows that this was not completed by June 1988, the time of the interview.

The foregoing were mainly technical problems, and all part of the learning curve. Advocates of global advertising claim that these problems diminish once they are understood and have become part of the creative guideline. One executive, however, introduced other, far-reaching problems that had an impact on local creative morale. These problems were less evident and more difficult to cope with:

> There is a group of people in this building, whose specialisation is creation of advertising. In global advertising that role is denied of you. For people on the ground, there is nothing for them to do. There is administration and probably odd translation, but nothing terribly creative. Even if they happen to be the lead agency, then there will be certain restraints imposed on them. Then we say 'Remember this is also for France, Germany and Switzerland'. That means compromise and they don't like it. They need a sense of freedom to execute what they want.

Yet another major problem was put forward by P. Nelson of McCann's, regarding costs and agency commissions:

> If a number of markets are going to show the same commercial, how much should each pay? Say we're shooting a film and it costs £150,000. Then we work out the share for Belgium and it comes to £50,000. Then Belgians come back and say it wouldn't cost them £50,000 if they did it themselves, because their production costs are different. That is only the beginning ...
>
> For example, three countries agree on the storyboard and the film is going to be an expensive one and cost £250,000 because one of the benefits of coming together is affording higher quality. So it is just over £80,000 each, but Finland says 'we are a small country, that is almost the size of our media budget'. The UK says 'we understand but we don't want to pay more than one third of the cost, because cost savings is one of the benefits'. They as the client ultimately have to work it out themselves.
>
> Then we have the problem on the agency side. We have three agencies in those three countries. They get commission on films they shoot. When the Finnish agency asks for its commission, we say 'we are shooting it in London, we have done most of the creative work, all the postproduction, we deserve it'. But the Finnish agency says 'it was in our annual budget and we need that commission'. So does the third country.
>
> So the problems are often less to do with the creative side but more to do with organisation and finances. Some clients are already addressing them, but solutions are not commonly applied yet. Then you ask yourself 'is it worth doing, if it brings more problems than it solves?'

R. Rippin of O & M expressed the same doubts on the client's side about how local marketing people react to global advertisements and its implications for the organisation. He said: 'These local affiliates quite rightly would say "How am I benefiting from this global advertising? We need to adapt your campaign for our market and also make a contribution to the centrally produced campaign. You are asking me to give away my authority and give money for it"'.

If neither agencies' nor clients' local branches were very excited about global advertising, and if some apparent benefits of it (such as cost savings) were not really what they were pretended to be, then why did global advertising continue to be so attractive to so many agencies and companies? The following extract shows that it was very much determined by clients' motives and decisions:

> Our client's Worldwide President said, 'we don't have a choice as our competitors are organised globally'. Therefore, our client says, 'what's the chance of survival, let alone winning, if we aren't organised in the same way?' It is almost like a religious concept. There is only one God and that is global marketing!

ADVERTISING TYPES AND GLOBAL CAMPAIGNS

Account executives' views about advertising that is more suitable for global campaigns are given in Table 8.2. The figures show that agencies believe, in the main, that ads with an 'emotional appeal' (that show different life-styles (vignettes)) and those that focus on 'product features' were easier to transfer. These two groups accounted for 66% of all replies.

Seven executives specified that 'testimonials' were difficult because they involved finding an internationally known celebrity. The ad's cast also needed to talk into the camera, which caused problems in translation and synchronisation. 'Comparison with competitors' and 'side-by-side comparisons' were banned in some European countries but encouraged in the USA. Companies had to have the same competitors in all the markets they operated in to be able to transfer such campaigns.

Four executives mentioned varying 'consumer needs' across countries as a factor that restricts this type of advertising. Three others remarked that advertising that stresses 'product features' should also take into consideration customer needs. Two interviewees said life-styles were tricky because different life-styles are not always acceptable in different local markets. However, the majority

Table 8.2 Advertising types more suitable for global campaigns as perceived by account executives

Easier-to-transfer advertising types	Frequency*	%*
Emotional appeal	18	46
Product features	16	41
Stressed visual aid	7	18
Side-by-side comparisons	6	15
Customer needs	3	8
Testimonials	1	3
Comparisons with competitors	—	—
Total	51	

Note
* Totals exceed the number of executives interviewed and 100% as it is a multi-response question.

believed that similar life-styles and emotions exist that appeal to all human beings, regardless of nationality: for example, a display of parental affection, eroticism and fear (as it was applied to the AIDS campaign). These general-appeal advertisements were usually enhanced by a 'visual hook' that strengthened the image and helped with recall, for example, a bouquet of flowers in Impulse advertisements or the use of a teddy bear in Comfort ads. These hooks were considered to be the company's 'properties', as effective ones were very difficult to find.

K. Rubie (Leo Burnett's Europe and Middle East Regional Managing Director) emphasised that advertisements that had less specific characteristics were easier to transfer because they had categorical benefits. Four other executives stressed the importance of the product itself in choosing the most suitable advertising type, together with the importance of the consumer target group and product strategy. These same executives also mentioned the unique selling preposition (USP), pointing out that this simplified the agency's task.

All the account executives contacted agreed that global campaigns should be visual, simple and factual. Image campaigns relied less on language, and did not require the use of pun or humour. P. Axten of McCann's concluded that transferable advertisements 'dealt with extrinsics, instead of getting into intrinsics. It is all to do with life-styles'. An executive from O & M said that global campaigns should be of a high quality and help with cost savings; campaigns that did not achieve these ends were discarded. For example, dialogue commercials (talking into camera) or commercials that required a local flavour were automatically eliminated.

GLOBAL CAMPAIGNS AND MARKETING-MIX ELEMENTS

In the initial agency questionnaire a comparative question was included that asked about the degree of standardisation or differentiation that was applied to the UK brand as opposed to its counterpart, which was promoted by the agency's HO (Question 1.5 in Appendix II). However, the first few interviews quickly revealed that agency–client relationships were very much client-led, and therefore not all global campaigns were transferred from agencies' head offices to local offices. Question 1.5 was, hence, not directly applicable to 25 of the 39 accounts. In the remaining 14 cases, the agency's HO was working with the clients' HQ in its home country. Campaign transfers were thus made from HO to the UK office.

When all successfully transferred campaigns were taken into consideration, certain common characteristics became apparent. The question was therefore rephrased, and the comparison was made for two brands that had a campaign transfer between them. One of these was strictly the UK brand, either as the global campaign donor or the receiver.

Table 8.3 The degree of standardisation applied to marketing-mix elements in successfully transferred global campaigns

Marketing-mix elements	Degree of standardisation
Crucial elements	
Product positioning	Total standardisation
Consumer target group	
End-use application	
Supplementary elements	
Brand name	High
Package type	
Package aesthetics	
Label	
Media available	
Media types used	
Pricing	
Marginal elements	
Pack sizes	Moderate
Brand relaunches/stage on PLC	
Advertising legislation	
Targeted market shares	Low
Competitors and expenditures	
Distribution channels	
Type and role of retailer	
Role and management of sales force	

After the degree of standardisation that was applied to each individual marketing-mix element of a specific brand was analysed, it was possible to regroup all marketing-mix elements into three categories. Table 8.3 displays this regrouping according to the degree of standardisation. The first group was classified as 'crucial elements'. These marketing-mix elements were either totally or almost totally standardised in the two countries that shared the same successful campaign. It was essential that these elements were standardised to ensure success. The second group was classified as 'supplementary elements'. These did not have to be totally standard for the campaign to be successful. In some cases they were highly standardised in both countries, in others they were not, but a high degree of standardisation in these elements was not a necessity. Last, the elements classified as 'marginal' made up the group where the highest degree of differentiation took place. The discrepancies observed in these elements did not hinder the success of the campaign. The degree of standardisation did not exceed 60%. In the last five elements of this group, the degree of standardisation was below 30%. These marginal elements were left to local management's judgement, as such factors were prone to local differences and hence required local adjustments.

It should be pointed out that the agency questionnaire did not include comparisons regarding product formula and product quality. The main reason for this was that these are totally product-related issues that do not require any input or involvement from the agency.

The results showed that standardisation of product positioning was crucial for the success of global campaigns, as were such attributes as the consumer target group and end-use applications, which were considered to be the tools to achieve specific product positioning. However, the findings also revealed one surprising result regarding 'pricing'. ('Pricing' means whether or not the brand was priced at a premium, par or below-par when compared to competitors' brands.) Although pricing was very much a part of product positioning, it was also seen as an element that had to be left to local management's discretion. Local operations were responsible for their own profitability; they were given autonomy in their pricing policy and they were held responsible for the consequences of their decisions. The following (from an agency executive) is a striking example of the importance of assessing product positioning, as it emphasises how powerful this is in transmitting the correct message to consumers:

> This brand is marketed in 17 countries with production sites in West Germany, France, Austria, UK, Canada, Australia and finally with three additional plants in the US. Although its positioning is unified, the product itself isn't! In 1964 ads were first produced in the UK. This same theme has been used in 17 markets for the last 18 years for different products with the same product positioning.

WHAT MATTERS MOST: HOT ADS OR HOT CAKES?

Of the interviewees, 55% stated that successful advertising should sell the client's products and that the agency's ultimate aim was to make money. Advertising was acknowledged as one of the most visible features of marketing but not the only element to affect sales. Two executives mentioned its positive impact on sales, on market share and in slowing down competitors' sales over time. However, this would not be a spontaneous change, and it was pointed out that success measured in terms of sales volume would not be consistent across different product groups. Although a high volume of sales was required for toothpastes, a smaller volume was acceptable for fragrances or other product groups that had high profit margins.

Only 36% of the executives stressed the importance of setting advertising objectives, referring to the measure of success as being the extent to which these objectives were fulfilled. However, fulfilling objectives as a measure of success was always mentioned as an adjunct to an increase in brand sales rather than in its own right. Creative excellence was suggested by 9%, although the interviewees demonstrated a degree of scepticism about this. Executives gave examples of advertisements that had won awards but that had not satisfied the client. Clients, usually, had reservations about very creative work: they wanted the brand name to be recalled, not the execution – advertising should not steal the show. An account director of O & M said that most clients looked at sales charts and then judged the advertisement subjectively: 'Do people in the company like it?' 'Does it manifest itself in our sales figures?' He also explained that, in the past, his agency defined and differentiated two sets of objectives: hard objectives were sales figures on a long-term basis (e.g. three years); soft objectives were consumers' positive attitudes towards the product and ways of improving their existing perceptions.

Having been asked for a definition of successful ads, executives were then asked whether or not they set advertising objectives before running campaigns. A total of 88% of respondents said that advertising objectives were determined jointly by the client and the agency. The remaining 12% implied that setting advertising objectives was done only by the client. One executive at McCann's hinted that, although objectives were set by the client, they reviewed these objectives with the client. The agency offered comments, saying whether or not the set objectives could be achieved within the allocated budgets. If there were too many objectives or too many vague ones, the agency interfered and asked for a reduction or clarification.

All in all, respondents indicated that their campaigns had predetermined advertising objectives, either set by the client or jointly with the agency. However, only 67% admitted that these same objectives were regularly referred to at the completion of the campaign. The remaining 33% said that the success of a campaign was not measured against the predetermined objectives, apart from certain exceptional cases. Account executives and clients seemed generally to rely on intangible measures, such as what the company's general manager thinks or what sort of reaction they receive from their sales force. It was very difficult, if not impossible, to isolate the effect of a single advertising campaign. Other, equally important, factors intervened in the entire process. Agencies also said that they received direct feedback from consumers if there was a complaint about the advertising (a misleading advertisement or a miscalculation in the advertisement). This is perhaps why they did not always refer diligently to previously set advertising objectives once the campaign was over: if something went wrong, they would no doubt be informed about it long before the campaign was over, for example, through a not very courteous phone call from the CEO of the client!

To sum up, we can confidently say that, today, ads that help the brand sell like hot cakes are still the ones very much desired and, rightly or wrongly, even expected. If they do not they are destined to be classed as 'not successful' in the eyes of clients and, unavoidably so, by agency executives.

REFERENCE

1. Rijkens, R. and Miracle, G. E. (1986) *European Regulation of Advertising*, Elsevier, Science Publishers, North-Holland.

9

YOUR CAMPAIGN HAS THE RIGHT TO BE GLOBAL, TOO!

We are back to our main topic: how to run successful global campaigns, which is no easy task but can be achieved if caution, care and know-how are applied. Practitioners should be aware of what they are letting themselves in for, and this means knowledge of and plenty of information about the client, the specific campaign, the country and other such details – no campaign will be successful if undertaken in ignorance. Executives in both corporates and agencies should be ultrasensitive to international clients and international campaigns. As Lewis Carroll put it, 'Take care of the sense and the sounds will take care of themselves' – in other words, common sense should prevail under all circumstances. Before describing how campaigns are co-ordinated in the international accounts handled by London agencies, we will briefly refresh our memories on the creation processes involved.

In Chapter 7 we saw how actual head offices (HOs) (lead agencies) would be involved in the creation of the account's advertising and even in its production, whereas official HOs would undertake more of an administrative role as the holding company. The actual HOs were usually assigned according to their proximity to the client's HQ, and they also co-ordinated accounts' advertising activities on a worldwide basis. However, these lead agencies did not necessarily create all the account's campaigns. Sometimes a particular job would be assigned to regional European co-ordination, if there was one. If a good campaign was spotted in a local market (market X) that could also be used in a different market (market Y), they then co-ordinated its transfer. In other cases the lead agency produced a specific campaign or transferred an already-developed one. All these factors explain why it was possible to see the use of various combinations of co-ordination methods that changed from company to company. There was also a mixing of methods in different accounts and different methods were even used for the different campaigns on the same account.

Although the co-ordination methods employed by each agency were not standard, it was still possible to observe certain patterns among the 39 accounts interviewed. First, all the transfers were made from the originating country to a country where it was believed that the campaign would run smoothly; in other words, the direction of transfer was not necessarily always from HO to other local offices. However, in the sample studied in this book, UK agencies were either the recipient or the originator of the campaign. F. Clementis of Foote Cone & Belding (FCB) stressed the actual HO's co-ordination role in the entire process: if they thought a specific campaign would be useful elsewhere, the HO drew the local office's attention to it. Another interesting point related to the campaign's originating office. This office acted as the 'custodian' of the campaign in all the countries in which it ran. For instance, one executive mentioned how the New York office was considered to be an 'ideas centre', even though HO was no longer located there, mainly because of historical links (although this office did assume the role of custodian for campaigns initiated by it). The same thing was experienced in the UK: if the UK office was the originator, then it became the custodian of that particular campaign – they became responsible for disseminating relevant information to other local offices that wanted to run it.

HOW TO CO-ORDINATE WHEN CREATING GLOBAL CAMPAIGNS

The three main approaches adopted by the London offices of international agencies when running global campaigns can be grouped as the lead-agency solution, the collaborative approach and the American Express approach. We will look at each approach in turn.

The Lead-Agency Solution

The lead-agency concept was observed in 90% of all the agencies contacted, but the style of the relationship they had with local offices varied, depending on the account and the client. Some lead agencies had a tight control over local offices whereas, in different accounts, they were considered to be advisers or vast data-banks to be consulted whenever the need arose. It would not, therefore, be misleading to say that, similar to clients, agencies were also found somewhere along the continuum from centralised to decentralised, and there were lead agencies of different hue all along this continuum. In its simplest form, lead agencies sought the following for their global campaigns:

Create → Transfer → Transliterate

A. Gledhill put it as follows:

> If we get a global brief, then we produce the ad in English. International Headquarters at Knightsbridge approves it and then we will send it to local agencies. 'Here is how TWA wants you to say it. How will you say it in your own language?' Once they transliterate it, they will send it to us and we will clear it with Knightsbridge. We will inform the local office. They will send us a copy for future reference. With the approval of their local clients, they will run it.

Local offices adhered to the general look, layout, style and tone of any given headline. They were expected to transliterate rather than translate. Local offices spent their time finding a good translation, not creating a new campaign, and this led to cost savings. G. Phillips of DDB on the American Airlines account stressed that, although the UK office created pan-European advertising, local agencies were responsible for local campaigns. Accordingly, the UK agency designed pan-European advertisements, avoiding the use of idioms, puns and other clever verbal communications. For example, it had recently used 'down to earth prices' in one of its advertisements. Although this worked well in Spanish, they had used the same picture but reworded it completely in French and German. The changes made by local offices were examined minutely by the UK office to ensure that the local versions remained faithful to the original layout, even down to the typeface. In the end, all the advertisements run in the different countries looked as if they were part of the same campaign.

Martini was another account that placed its worldwide advertising with a UK lead agency. However, the role this lead agency played in this account was quite different from others, and this brings us to the centralised lead-agency approach. Martini is an Italian, family-owned business based in Turin, and it was very much centralised in its approach to advertising. Only two men took decisions on worldwide advertising. There was a Group Board Chairman, who was a member of the Rossi family. He was also the board's nominated advertising man. The Group Board Chairman also had an International Marketing/Advertising Director, who collaborated with him. Hence the agency had the simple job of selling the advertising to only those two men. As P. Nelson put it 'No committees, no democracy!' Presentations to country managers were 'for information'. Since the decisions had already been made, any selling was 'cosmetic'.

In the agency, three people led the account. Every single detail would be discussed and agreed between the agency and the client, even down to the lengths of different commercials. Basic film costs comprised the location, the crew, shooting the film and producing opticals in the laboratory. Once that was done, making cuts to produce different lengths of the same commercial did not add much extra cost. Martini, Italy, paid for the basic film production costs, and local clients paid for any adaptations needed. Agency commissions were calculated by taking a certain fixed percentage of the production or adaptation costs made. The UK agency hence received more commission than any of the local offices. Once approved, the film was produced and sent to 26 countries around the globe, with the instruction, 'This is the new film. Please use it as soon as possible'.

The Rossi family was dedicated to global advertising: they insisted that their advertising had the same look across countries. Even the music used in TV commercials had not changed since 1971. However, they used different arrangements of the same melody – from ballad to jazz to disco. If local Martini clients were not satisfied with the advertisement, they registered their complaint with their HQ. If Turin agreed it was a valid complaint, they incorporated that point into the brief for their next commercial. P. Nelson said:

> It is a dictatorship and that's why it works. It is good for the agency because it gets us out of all the hassle of trying to sell the work to different people and makes a very satisfactory relationship. It works simply because the client understands that he himself has to make it work.

Another executive gave a different example of an HO–lead-agency relationship. In this, the UK agency had developed an animated advertisement to the UK client's satisfaction. However, the client's HQ had stopped the UK office from using another UK-originated campaign, mainly because the UK agency had recently produced commercials for many brands, some of which had also been used for the first time in the USA. The UK client was told to use an Italian commercial for the brand's launch instead of its own. Although centralised, this was a very different HO–lead-agency relationship from Martini's. In the latter example, a fair chance of campaign development in local offices is implied and, in this way, local creatives were not deprived of becoming involved in new developments. It also shows concern for local offices' commissions. Put bluntly, monopolising campaign development to a few locations would have a detrimental effect on other offices' budgeted incomes.

Having looked at the centralised lead-agency approach we now turn to the other end of the continuum. Here, the UK offices' association with their respective lead agencies was more liberated and less confining. The relationship was more of a liaison rather than a taking of directives. These accounts had the flexibility of being able to choose two or three films from among the fifteen to twenty produced annually by their lead agencies. Such brands, essentially, wanted to adhere to their American image and background. It was not possible for them to achieve the same high quality of commercials with their UK budgets and so, therefore, using a US-originated commercial suited them perfectly. All new material produced by the USA was sent to the local offices. After examining these, the local offices made the first contact and asked for the transfer.

One agency executive expressed the nature of the relationship as follows: 'The Head Office has the liberty to scream over the phone and say it is wrong and get into debate with us, but they have no direct control'.

In a different example, the agency had two separate teams in two different locations. Their account management team for the client was in one city, their creative team in another. However, both teams were in the USA. Instead of writing the brief for the agency's London office, the UK client wrote to the account management team in the USA. Everything this team produced had to be sold to the UK client. Again, twelve to fifteen commercials were produced centrally each year, and the UK client chose three or four from among them. The agency's London office handled the changes the UK client asked for, such as making the music track more upbeat or making a different cut for a 20 second instead of a 30 second commercial.

From studying these examples it is clear that lead agencies and the bonds they have with their local offices differ vastly, and this is again a consequence of their clients' organisational structures and specific needs on specific accounts.

This will be examined in more detail later; we need first to extend our investigation into the different approaches employed by looking at the second suggested solution: the 'collaborative approach'.

The Collaborative Approach

In the collaborative approach, if the account was handled by the same agency in more than one country then the agency drew on more than one agency's resources. The same brief was sent to the different local offices and each developed its own campaign ideas. The individual ideas were presented to a jury of creative directors of local offices. The work that received the most votes was allowed to develop fully for presentation to the client. Examples given by executives will help to clarify this approach. One account executive explained the process as follows:

> We try to persuade our client to use more than one of our offices. Choosing specific offices to do the same work is my expertise, depending on what they are good at. A lot also depends on simple things like the work load in that specific office at the moment. It is very tempting always to use the London office, as you are running it on your doorstep. You also think who or which office will be good at doing that particular type of campaign. Sometimes you might choose an office struggling for a while to impress a local client. To raise their profile within International Headquarters, I would then pick them up. So a lot of factors have an impact on choosing the agency.
>
> Once you get the agency, you send them an advertising brief or have a meeting brief with them. Then roughly you leave two thirds of the time you have got for creative development. Once you reach that stage, you pull together creative directors from each office to a central location. They go through their work, present it to each other. They make recommendations and vote which one should go. At their level of seniority, they don't battle it out. They are very professional. There would also be a European creative director to chair those meetings and act as an ombudsman. Towards the end, after they finish storyboards, presentation roughs, they come back with two campaigns this time. Creative directors will choose one. Then we go to the client and say 'you have paid for two campaigns and here they are. We recommend A'. We will present as many as the client pays for.

One of the executives interviewed gave another example that had recently occurred with one of their international clients. This shows how they joined forces with other European offices for pan-European advertising. The UK office was the lead agency. This office briefed the Zurich, Milan, Paris, Frankfurt and London creative teams for a TV commercial. Those five offices came back with 21 executions. These 21 were cut down to 6. These were presented to the client and put into research. Finally, the Swiss alternative was chosen, with a great deal of co-operation from the other European creatives. As the lead agency, the London office dealt with European co-ordination, which co-ordinated each local affiliate's advertising. Although the commercial was acceptable in all the markets it was researched, it worked better in the UK, Switzerland and West Germany. Another complicating factor was that the Swiss team did not have a TV department, so the film was subcontracted to an independent producer in the UK in order to make it more international.

This method was also observed in other agencies. For example, Mr Rippin of Ogilvy & Mather (O & M) said that when the UK office was the lead office they co-produced campaigns with other offices, such as West Germany, Holland, Belgium and France. This was especially so if they had a particularly difficult task – they would start the offices simultaneously to increase the chances of coming up with the right solution. In his words, 'This is a fairly standard practice'.

The following approach is actually an improved and more organised version of the collaborative approach, and it is practised by American Express. Although it has flexibility for local adaptations, local offices' inputs are co-ordinated from the European HO. This office also undertakes the central execution of campaigns. The method, therefore, is named after American Express as an acknowledgement of their pioneering work in this area.

The American Express Solution

To understand this approach, it is necessary to give some background to the American Express account. In 1962, O & M acquired the American Express account in the USA. Over the next twenty-five years it grew tremendously, covering 38 countries in addition to six O & M offices that handled US operations. In 1987 they were O & M's biggest client. The account was handled at the most senior level of management in both the client and the agency, both of which were headed by their worldwide presidents. There was a total match of agency and client at all levels, including regional and functional divisions. These relationships were agreed by the mutual consent of both companies.

Clear guidelines were set for organisational structure, the account management team and for new campaign developments. These were treated as commandments and were hence strictly adhered to, each office making a concerted effort to abide by them. The procedures set out for a new campaign development are listed below to highlight their style, precision and coherence:

- Every office will strictly adhere to the official worldwide positioning statement for each product. If an exception to this is being considered, agreement to the change in positioning or strategy must be received from O & M, New York and from American Express, New York before any creative development is initiated.
- Each office will always ask 'Is there an existing international campaign that fulfils the brief?'
- Each office will check with O & M, New York and with the appropriate Regional Co-ordinator to determine what experience we have on the subject.
- Each office will send to O & M, New York and the appropriate Regional Co-ordinator, copies of all major new advertising work at an early creative stage including strategy/briefing document, copy, layouts and storyboards. Material can be sent after local client approval of strategy and concept, but sufficient time should be allowed for comment.

Historically, most campaigns had originated in the USA, with local executions. They had a well-liked and well-known 'Do you know me?' (DYKM) campaign. This was first introduced into Europe in Italy in 1983–4. This campaign idea had been initiated in the USA twelve years previously, and the idea was to show very well-known personalities by name but not by face, for example, Mr Sony, Mr Benetton and Mr Reagan jr. Although the concept was strong, the major drawback was in finding suitable personalities. Executions were made on a local basis, with a different script and different personalities and, where personalities were internationally known, they were used across countries. In terms of economies of scale and cost savings not much was gained. Mr Benetton's commercial was closest to a pan-European DYKM and was one of the few that worked in most markets. Having found the right personality, there were then certain technical problems, for instance, convincing those personalities to participate, fixing a date for filming and, finally, how good the personalities were when it came to acting before a camera – all of which were never easy!

After twelve years of DYKM in the USA, it was decided that a new creative campaign was essential. In addition to the existing team, all the other teams in the New York office that had never worked on the account were assigned to work on the new campaign. One of the new teams came up with the 'membership' idea by looking at the American Express card itself. On the card it said 'member since . . .', and a date was given, similar to being a member of a club. Membership also had certain privileges.

The membership campaign was launched early in 1987 in the USA and card acquisitions increased enormously. Because the campaign was so successful in the USA, the President of American Express for Europe decided to launch the same campaign in Europe in January 1988. It was September by now, and the UK office only had four months to finalise preparations. The major hurdle the London office faced was adapting the US-originated membership campaign for Europe, mainly because some vignettes in the campaign were very American. This was especially true of France, where American advertising is generally resented. They therefore kept the format for the beginning and end but added local vignettes in the middle. In the following quotation we see how this was realised. From the sound of it, it definitely seemed a challenge:

> Each of the vignettes were emphasising one major benefit-service of American Express, like 24-hour card replacement, local utility of the card. We said to all the local markets that we are going to reshoot some of the vignettes that looked too American. Let us know which ones won't work in your market. Most agreed on some vignettes as being unsuitable.
>
> So we made a list of replacements and then asked for new ideas. Then all of us got together making a list of new vignettes, specifying which market is interested in which vignette. However, we ended up with too many new vignettes. Therefore, we combined similar scenes. We had only one restaurant setting instead of three. We had one big meeting with the client and all creatives to reach a final decision on vignettes, sets, casting country by country. Then we made local offices sign a contract, because they change their minds during or after the shooting. It happened with DYKM. Then we had a problem of splitting up costs. It wouldn't be fair to divide by the number of countries. It would be unfair on small markets like Austria. Therefore, we divided by current cards.
>
> We shot in London, with different vignettes for seven countries. We kept the set, but changed the actors one after the other. All had to be done in one day. We had enormous cost savings from production. However, it wasn't easy to please all the

creatives. There were also difficulties at technical level. Newly added vignettes shouldn't stand out in terms of tone and grading of the commercial. We had to make sure that colour was uniform. We also took different cuts of the same commercial for 30 second, 45 second or 60 second lengths, according to specific needs of each local market. In most cases, post-production – mixing, dubbing, synchronising – was done in local markets.

Another problem we faced was with local creatives. In the past with DYKM they had high involvement. They had done all the script and the execution. But in a centrally produced campaign, they don't do anything apart from adapting the copy. To motivate local offices and boost their morale, we decided to split jobs among different offices. Each time we have a new assignment, we'll give it to a different market. The next one is assigned to Italy. It already started working. Other markets are also being less difficult, knowing it will be their turn the next time!

That is one thing about American Express. They always make us feel as their marketing partners. They don't give us just briefs. We are very much involved from the very early stages of a new concept, even launch of a new service. Same applies to local O & M offices. They have to feel a part of a team. Then, you get their co-operation as well. At the end, without comprising on the production quality, we have been able to save American Express some money. So that's probably why they were so pleased.

R. Steward of McCann's mentioned a similar practice for Unilever's Frozen Foods. However, it was not possible to obtain very detailed information on actual campaign development. Interestingly, he also emphasised involving local offices and creative teams in the earlier stages of preproduction in order to overcome any anticipated problems. He stressed that emotional problems can play a major role when dealing with global campaigns.

In a nutshell, the advantages of the American Express solution could be summarised as follows:

- Cost savings in production.
- A better-quality commercial.
- Local involvement of O & M offices at the early stages of preproduction.
- Motivation of local O & M offices.
- Local sensitivity by using suitable vignettes in every market.
- Building upon HQ/HOs' experience and knowledge ('not reinventing the wheel', 'not starting from scratch').
- Close HQ/HO contact with their affiliates and local offices.
- No detrimental effects on local offices' budgeted commissions.

However, it should also be emphasised that the American Express solution required an immense amount of co-ordination, the organisation of the European office, the collaboration of local offices and predetermined coherent guidelines by agency and client heads. It also needed previous experience in global advertising activities, with a long transition period. For example, in the American Express example, the DYKM campaign was used as a stepping-stone for their true globalisation efforts before running the first pan-European membership campaign. They managed to attain all the advantages of global advertising, which counteracted any of its drawbacks. It should also be mentioned that the American Express approach survived all the major problems cited in Chapter 8.

DEVELOPING GLOBAL CAMPAIGNS FOR APPLES AND ORANGES

As has already been said at the beginning of this chapter, global campaigns were not necessarily transferred from HO to other local offices. In some cases they were produced by the lead agency, or European co-ordination produced them to be used in multimarkets. At other times and with less centralised clients, local agencies created advertisements for running in their local markets. As was mentioned previously, although these campaigns were not developed intentionally for multimarket use, if they captured the interest of one of the co-ordinating bodies, they were transferred to other local markets.

All in all there are both decentralised and centralised clients – just as there are apples and oranges, and the one is not better than the other. It is simply a matter of taste. In a similar way, there is nothing wrong with a decentralised or centralised client or working with such clients. What *is* wrong is to compare them. Another common mistake is to treat these dissimilar things in the same fashion: apples might be better in a crumble pie, whereas oranges are more suitable for juice-extraction. The same thing holds true for clients who have different corporate cultures and unique ways of looking at business life.

Agencies should understand fully their client's business philosophy. Having found out which category their clients are in, then suitable campaign transfers can be considered. For decentralised clients, global campaigns mainly come to life by coincidence. At the other extreme, however, centralised clients develop international campaigns wilfully from the very start.

Let's take a closer look at decentralised clients and campaigns. First these campaigns were not produced to a global brief. The execution of these campaigns were left to local markets. If adaptation was required after the transfer to different markets then each market made its own changes. The originating office would receive commissions as the campaign producer and developer. The other local offices acquired their commissions through the alterations they had made to make the campaign fit the local market. The whole process was less planned, less organised and less co-ordinated. A few examples that fall into this category include the following:

- Colgate Palmolive's commercial for Palmolive soap that was originated in 1985 by FCB Venezuela and run in twenty to twenty-five countries.
- Timotei shampoo, which was produced by Elida Gibbs for a Swedish launch in 1975 as a cinema commercial. It was subsequently run in twenty-five countries.
- J. Walter Thompson (JWT), Brazil, developed a campaign for Kodacolor Gold Color Film, which was subsequently used not only in Latin America but also in Japan, South East Asia, and six European countries.

On the other hand, in global or pan-European campaigns, the parties involved knew from the very beginning that they were aiming for a worldwide campaign, and the campaign idea was usually the end result of local offices' collaborative efforts. As this required more direction from HQ/HO or other co-ordinating bodies, the distribution of commissions was more complex. Sometimes local offices took turns in producing different campaigns, as in the American Express example. Mostly, however, they operated on a fee basis: the clients paid a basic fee for each alternative creative solution they had asked for. Hence each office that was assigned the job was paid a set fee. If one alternative was produced, then local offices received their commission for transliteration, post-production or any other minor changes they made, such as adapting the music track or the voice-over. Any adaptations that were needed for different local markets were itemised before production commenced. Such adaptations (for example, making different cuts for different commercial lengths or filming different versions of the same square to allow for variations in legislation) were executed according to guidelines that were set articulately from the very start (these two types of campaign development are summarised in Table 9.1).

The two styles reflect the clients' corporate cultures as, in all the 13 agencies contacted, it was possible to find accounts that belonged to both groups. Hence the style was dictated by the client, not the agency, which mirrored the client's culture in its own structure. Groups of accounts exhibited different degrees of centralisation: although they all lay at the same end of the continuum in the same region, each had its own unique territory within that area.

It should be emphasised that neither approach is superior to the other: the structure of each client and each campaign development was unique – as distinct and incomparable as apples and oranges.

Table 9.1 Global campaign development styles and corporate cultures – a comparison of decentralised and centralised approaches

Decentralised (coincidental global campaigns)	Centralised (wilfully designed global campaigns)
A local campaign brief	A global brief
Local creation and execution	Collaborative campaign development
Adaptations made locally	Adaptations incorporated into the central execution
Commissions received according to each office's contribution (i.e. originator country receives more)	Central production by different local offices taking turns, or payment made on a fee basis, or each office receives commissions for its transliteration and post-production efforts
Less HO/HQ direction and contribution	More HO/HQ direction and contribution
A less centralised corporate culture	A more centralised corporate culture
Less systematic and planned	More systematic and deliberately planned

ALTER LESS, BLUNDER LESS

When investigating campaigns that were successfully transferred to the UK, did a pattern of adaptation emerge? Were the changes that were made drastic or minor? Were particular elements always altered and others left untouched? From our interviews it appears that adaptations were kept to the minimum to reduce production costs: elements were not altered unless it was absolutely necessary to do so. If an ad needed its general theme to be altered before it was run in a different country, then using it did not lead to any gains over producing a new campaign. Such elements as general theme, typography, colour, type and quality of material, layout and pictorial images were not changed.

Slight changes were made in the dimensions of point-of-purchase materials and press ads, in the jingle used as well as in the copy and execution. Such changes involved adapting the music track or using the same one with an upbeat, or altering the sound track or voice-over. Sometimes the commercial's name was changed: for example, Apple's commercial was called 'Red Eye' in America, implying that a flight from the West coast to the East was against the sun; in the UK it was renamed 'Overnight to Heathrow'. Changes were sometimes made to the slogan. Michael J. H. Constantine (Regional Account Management Director of Leo Burnett, Regional HQ) explained that 7UP's US slogan was 'Feel So Good/Coming Down', where rain was used to communicate its refreshment benefit. In the UK 'Feel So Good/Cooling Down' was used, as it was believed that cooling down would better convey 7UP's 'refreshment' strategy. A secondary concern was the chance of misinterpretation of the US slogan. Similar modifications were also common in end-lines; in a chewing-gum ad the original pay-off line was 'It keeps you humming'. However, it was remarked that 'humming' had body-odour connotations and the line was, therefore, corrected. In addition, wherever packs were different, pack shots were changed.

All these changes involved editing and were not major. Translations or transliterations were, on the other hand, left entirely to local markets where offices were expected to spend their time looking for transliterations of copy that would sound good in the local language. Another element that varied from one market to another was the use of different-length commercials. In the USA, 45 second and 60 second ads were mainly used, whereas in Europe 30 second and 45 second ones were more common. However, different commercial lengths were supplied by the campaign's originating country, and local offices used whichever length(s) they wanted instead of reshooting the entire film.

Adaptations made to global campaigns were, therefore, not drastic (one of the prerequisites of global campaigns). If they were substantial they defeated the whole object of globalisation. P. Axten of McCann's said that 'One has to bear in mind the question of "is it really critical?" Otherwise you can easily outspend the initial cost of shooting a new film just by making adaptations'.

DOES ANYONE NEED SATELLITE TV FOR GLOBAL CAMPAIGNS?

Of the 39 account executives interviewed, only 21 were asked about satellite TV, as this is a recent development still in its infancy. These executives were asked about satellite TV's prospects for global advertising. All agreed that satellite TV was, in fact, still very new, with only a 2% coverage across Europe (the interviews were completed by June 1988). However, it was anticipated that it would become more widely available in the coming years and not just confined to being received by big hotels. It was also anticipated that specific target groups (such as business people) would be accessible in the near future. All saw satellite TV's future as promising, rosy and rather as an inevitable fact of life, although it needed time to develop more fully. T. Symington of Harrisons said that satellite TV might even help to lower the current TV airing rates by creating competition. F. Clementis of FCB pointed out that the new media will not move the emphasis away from local companies: it will be additional support, not a substitute for local advertising.

If satellite TV received such wide acceptance by agency executives, what were the prerequisites for using it? Were there any conditions that had to be fulfilled before starting to use it? To begin with, brands had to communicate with a uniform message to the same consumer groups for the same usage and in the same product positioning before they could even be considered for satellite TV. One executive admitted that, initially, they selected four brands of a major international client for satellite. These four brands were reduced to two, as the other two were not uniform in their marketing strategies across Europe. F. Clementis gave the example of Ajax, which had a different UK positioning from the rest of Europe and this, hence, impeded its use on satellite TV. It was also pointed out that, when placing commercials on satellite TV, a lead agency had to be assigned for each account to enable central media buying. Furthermore, messages had to be consistent: executives recommended the use of simple English, with minimal spoken words and humour. Messages had to be enhanced by visuals, and have a musical impact. Five interviewees said that the new medium will increase HO involvement, as it will necessitate more co-ordination and a harmonisation of action rather than the employment of individual units. However, it was also forecast that the extensive use of satellite TV would not come about before 1992, as brands have not yet been promoted uniformly in Europe.

At the moment, views on the Single Market and its effects on satellite TV cannot really go beyond speculation (the latest stages of the Single Market and advertising were mentioned in Chapter 4). As will be recalled, the October 1989 Broadcasting Directive (harmonising member states' laws on advertising by removing existing barriers) has been accepted. Although this directive contains measures to implement this, discrepancies in legislation are still wide-spread. Until legislation is harmonised, companies cannot be expected to standardise their brands (from packaging to product formula) across EEC countries. The criteria mentioned by executives as suitable brands on satellite TV resembled those mentioned for the marketing-mix elements of global campaigns (the standardisation of these is covered in Chapter 8).

The comments made about satellite TV could act as a checklist for both agencies and advertisers when they assess their brands' readiness for 1992. Until now, global campaigns were pursued at the discretion of each individual company. However, this freedom of choice will be regulated and shaped by the EEC's efforts to harmonise Europe into a Single Market. Such a checklist is included at the end of Chapter 10 (the 'Magic Checklist'), based on the findings of this research.

10
CONCLUDING REMARKS

THE AGENCY–CLIENT DILEMMA

The aim of this book has been to look at agency head office (AHO) involvement in global advertising practices. Account executives invariably mentioned their clients and their clients' HQs first, instead of their own HOs, which initially seemed mere coincidence. However, further investigation revealed that the degree of involvement was very much determined by the client's corporate culture. Within the same agency, very decentralised or centralised accounts were found. Agencies reorganised themselves to accommodate the needs of the client. The way clients organised themselves and their affiliates affected the extent of HQ involvement in their own affiliates and, indirectly, in their agencies. Thus AHO involvement in local agency branches varied from one account to another.

Agency–client relationships have never remained static; they evolve and, in the long term, are transformed by the actions of the client. Examples of these changes are given in Chapter 6. Most agencies have branches in different continents because their major clients also have subsidiaries there (1, 2). Miracle (3) points out that the client's degree of centralised control in international advertising determines how the agency is organised. How the agency expands to acquire international networks varies: there is no 'best' method, since circumstances change because of the agency's characteristics and its client list. Adding support to the findings given in the present book, M. Skinner, Hong Kong Office Director of DDB International, has said (4, p. 63) 'We are not here to make short term profits. We're here for network reasons. If we're not in Asia, we're not going to be considered by clients in New York and London'.

O'Connor (5) stresses that, in international marketing, agencies can only be as good as their clients permit, again emphasising that clients lead the agency–client relationship. McCann-Erickson (6) state that global brand management takes many forms and styles: it is possible to find clients at any degree of standardisation on the 'soft' and 'hard' co-ordination continuum, as shown in Table 10.1. McCann-Erickson also admit that none of their 41 international accounts lies at the same point of this continuum, although the agency is the same. Miracle (3) says that no company is identical to another: company histories, product lines, management orientation and other internal factors vary widely. Two major forces, therefore, exert pressure on agencies' internationalisation processes: the globalisation of markets and the need to follow clients (7, 8). Therefore, whether it be the internationalisation of agencies (7, 8), establishing new branches (2) or the issue of agency commissions (9), the client's influence on agencies is paramount.

THE CLIENT'S COMMITMENT TO GLOBAL CAMPAIGNS

Agency executives repeated over and over again that the client must be well organised and well prepared before running global campaigns: the client had to have line authority over its affiliates to ensure the centrally produced campaign was run, otherwise the agency could not possibly guarantee the local client's co-operation. Agencies become frustrated by clients who want to use international advertising but who are organisationally unprepared for it (10, 11, 12). T. Bannister (Saatchi & Saatchi's (S & S) Joint Chief Executive Officer) is quoted as saying that globalisation will not work unless clients learn to centralise their own strategy (13). Stressing the same point, the Vice-Chairman of McCann-Erickson, B. Day, states that when clients are unprepared to execute a global concept, the agency will have to fight local operations in every campaign. He adds (14, p. 38) that the

> Client says to the agency 'Keep your boys in line. We have to keep our boys in line'. So you need a manufacturer who has an organisation he can control and chooses to control, regionally and in individual offices and an agency that matches it. And to get all those ducks in a row is horrendous. It happens from time to time but it is extremely difficult.

Organisational structure, the size of the manufacturer and the agency itself are all important when a standardised approach is applied (15). The 'corporate organisation of the advertiser' is also listed among the factors that determine the appropriateness of uniform advertising (16): if a company is organised to conduct business on a multinational basis and it has control of its subsidiaries, advertising transfers are said to be easier.

To sum up, although client and local-management support is an obvious precondition for running smooth global campaigns, this is rarely the case in reality.

Table 10.1 The 'soft'–'hard' co-ordination continuum used as a tool when managing brands across countries

Experience	Strategy	Concept	Campaign	Advertising	Execution	Material
Cross-border information flow only	Sharing the same basic brand strategy	Testing the same brand proposition	Developing a standard, co-ordinated campaign	Using the same pattern material or brand property	Centralised production	Local campaign produced and placed from the centre
'Soft' co-ordination						*'Hard' co-ordination*

(*Source*: Reference 6.)

THROUGH INVOLVEMENT COMES CONTROL

Of the 39 accounts studied in this book, 60% of the executives said they had a 'high' degree of HO involvement in the creation and production of advertising. 'High' AHO involvement accounts were encountered when:

- the AHO also handled the account in the client's home country; and
- these accounts belonged to corporates where a high degree of HQ involvement was exercised within the client's organisation.

Once again, the client's organisational structure was the determining factor. The remaining 40% stated that they had relatively less involvement. 'Low' AHO involvement accounts had some features in common, as follows:

- These accounts were either not handled by the same AHO in the client's home country or the specific product or service was not marketed in the client's home country.
- The agency's London office acted as regional (European) co-ordination or controlled the account totally from London. Therefore it received either less involvement from European co-ordinators or it itself (as the UK office) was the European co-ordinator or lead agency.

AHO involvement increased whenever the UK office (as a local branch) was faced with a crisis.

Practitioners are warned about the misuse of international campaigns as hasty decisions: if neither the client nor the agency are prepared for it, the consequences for both can be very damaging. For example, one paper (17) draws attention to local clients in decentralised companies: local clients may be so hostile to any international development that even a communication of intent is difficult. This suggests that the 'not-invented-here' syndrome means much more: not-informed-here, not-involved-here, not-impressed-here, not-international-here and not-invoiceable-here. The last item has far-reaching repercussions for local branches, as Chapter 8 has shown. It has also been suggested (18) that the not-invented-here syndrome is too simple an idea, and that it should be examined in detail, as it involves career-path motivations and personal-income incentives. Agency fees and the adverse feelings of local creative directors (who cannot include centrally produced campaigns in their portfolios of creative work) are also cited as major hurdles that need to be overcome in global campaigns. Some authors go so far as to suggest that, sometimes, local executives create these obstacles in order to prevent outside control in their activities, or to cater to local pride in ownership (19). However, not surprisingly this is not advised, as such a trick would lead to an increase in HQ involvement.

Conflict between HQs and local operations are inevitable and, to a certain extent, desirable—as Wiechmann and Pringle (20) have noted. The tension and friction that exists between them should not be misinterpreted: these separate organisations should act as catalysts, not hindrances to smooth campaign transfers, having the same objectives to enable them to work in harmony towards a given end and to produce cost-effective results.

THE ORGANISATIONAL SET-UP AND GLOBAL CAMPAIGNS

Peebles and Ryans (21) stress that the lead-agency concept (see Chapter 7) can work well for some clients, but that it works best for those that happen to be in the same market as the agency's home office. They suggest that the lead agency underplays its own home office as an international client-control point and that, instead, the client's international agency co-ordination and quality and service supervision in all the markets that serve the client are the responsibility of the lead agency or the local agency office that initially acquired the account. These authors also warn that each local agency may be at a different stage of international expertise; therefore, all lead agencies may not be able to handle accounts with the same efficiency. Interestingly, Peebles and Ryans (*ibid.*) do not differentiate official and actual HOs, as the present study has done. They suggest that the lead-agency concept works best if the client's HQ happens to be in the same city as the agency's HO. This study, however, suggests that agencies no longer leave this to coincidence but assign the local agency closest to the client's HQ as the lead agency.

On the other hand, not all agencies favour the lead-agency concept. For example, E. Roncarelli (Foote Cone & Belding's (FCB) President of the Multinational Business Group) stated in an interview (12) that FCB resists the nomination of specific lead countries that have the greatest experience with a particular client and the greatest resources: this would mean that creativity is monopolised in a couple of markets, hence alienating other local offices that have fewer resources. The solution offered in this book (the American Express approach in Chapter 9) invalidates these suggested drawbacks of lead agencies: they should therefore be considered more seriously by agency executives.

Furthermore, it has been shown here that it is not uncommon to find local agency branches that have been established specifically for particular clients. The Volkswagen example, given by G. Phillips of DDB Needham (Chapter 7), has also been cited elsewhere (22, p. 241): 'The Volkswagen advertising in America was handled very successfully by Doyle Dane Bernbach. When this American Agency opened an office in Germany, the Volkswagen company dropped its national agency there and gave the Account in Germany to the German office of Doyle Dane Bernbach'.

In addition official HOs were determined by ownership, but they did not become involved in creative development unless the client's HQ happened to be in the same city as the official HO. Official and actual HOs' duties then overlapped and they were undertaken by the same office. Also, local branches usually reported to official HOs on financial issues.

The key factor in deciding whether to establish regional HOs for Europe was, in all the agencies interviewed, the client. However, as the quotations in Chapter 7 show, agency executives wanted to keep their regional HOs at arm's length (if they possibly could): if they did not show resentment towards them, they certainly had reservations. The local agency's size was also a critical factor in determining how they reacted to the advice they received from their regional HOs; while smaller agencies welcomed regional HOs help, larger agencies rejected it completely.

Miracle (3) (agreeing with this study) points out that some agencies have no overseas regional co-ordinating office, while others have several. The number of regional offices, Miracle says, will increase as the agencies expand, the regional co-ordinating offices usually serving as a channel of communication between the regional agencies and the HO. Regional offices also supervise new business developments and monitor the quality of advertising and staffing levels.

Naylor (17) gives practitioners' views of worldwide management supervisors ('WMS' in Ogilvy & Mather's (O & M) jargon), indicating that in O & M these supervisors are considered to be friendly diplomats or ambassadors who travel the world, 'lubricating' client relationships and drawing attention to good ideas or pitfalls. He observes that a WMS needs to be mature, have common sense and a likeable personality. The WMS will then be listened to and, in return, be influential. Bernstein seems to agree with the account executives interviewed for this book on the role of international executives: one of the executives who was interviewed called them 'international seagulls' (see Chapter 7), while Bernstein calls them 'international fire fighters' with a touch of the arsonist in them (23, p. 133):

> These corporate executives manipulated the world like puppet masters, much of the time blithely unaware that the strings had been cut. Occasionally the international executive would pack his battle plan and a couple of drip-dry shirts and go see. He would settle little local problems and wing away. International fire fighter they called him back at base. But he knew he also had to be something of an arsonist if he was ever to justify a return trip.

Other sources acknowledge regional offices as pragmatic efforts in the move towards faster and smoother global marketing strategies (24). It would, therefore, not be incorrect to say 'We cannot live with or without regional offices'. Regional HOs and their client counterparts need to be investigated further in order to understand them fully and for their roles to be justified.

THE 'MIRRORING EFFECT'

As was discussed in Chapter 7 (see Figure 7.1), in order to be able to give the best service to their clients, agencies mirrored their clients' organisational structures. Three links were identified – with the lead agency; with the official HO; and with the agency–client relationship (25):

1. Administrative links between the AHO and the local UK office (for example, reporting on financial issues).
2. Links for the creation/production/transfer of campaigns between the UK agency and the agency assigned the role of lead agency for a specific account. Lead agencies were assigned according to their proximity (in the international network) to the client's HQ. They generated a considerable flow of creative input between local offices. These administrative and creation/production/transfer links were replicated at corresponding levels in the client's structure.
3. Clients had 'shadows' in their agencies at each level of seniority, with corresponding responsibilities and titles.

Miracle (3) has shown that, when a client has a high degree of centralised control, some agencies will appoint one person or perhaps a team to co-ordinate and control all the campaigns in a given region. Interestingly, Rijkens (26, p. 20) specifies that

> In order to be able to co-ordinate, guide and control the agency work for a multinational advertiser, the international agency must be organised in such a way that the authority it can exert over its branches will match the authority of the advertiser over his affiliates. In other words, the agency must be able to provide the multinational advertiser with an organisation which is the reflected image of his own. This can vary from a rather loosely co-ordinated operation to one which is almost entirely controlled from the centre. The key word is flexibility.

Although Miracle (3) has suggested that no two companies are alike, companies should choose an agency 'that most nearly meets its own particular requirements'. Over the past twenty years or so, international agencies have become very flexible and very much client-led (the 'mirroring effect') – most probably as a result of fierce international advertising competition. This symbiotic relationship between agencies and their international clients evolves as changes take place in each organisation's structure.

As international clients devote huge advertising budgets to their worldwide marketing activities, agencies do not attempt to change the client's way of doing business but try, instead, to understand and work around the parameters the client has established. 'Working effectiveness' is another reason for matching: if the client has divided itself up into North and South Europe, and the agency has divided itself into Scandinavia, Central Europe and the Mediterranean, responsibilities could overlap leading to confusion. A less rational reason for matching is to secure the smooth conduct of business, the agency demonstrating good will and courtesy to the client in meeting its requirements.

GIVING OUR COMMITMENT TO GLOBAL CAMPAIGNS

Of the agencies included in this book, 43% of the executives interviewed had 'positive' attitudes towards global advertising, whereas 57% had reservations. Not surprisingly, those account executives who had frequently transferred campaigns were the ones who had positive feelings (see Chapter 8), and a wide range of factors were given to support their views. Those who had reservations generally agreed that successful campaigns were the exception rather than the rule, claiming that such campaigns led to compromises and that advertisers had to be satisfied with the lowest common denominators in each market. G. M. Black, Chairman of J. W. Thompson's (JWT) Frankfurt office, is quoted as saying (4, p. 65) 'If I were to make a film for Europe-wide distribution, by the time we went through all the rules governing national advertising, we would be left with a poster!' This demonstrates clearly what is meant by the 'lowest common denominator'!

One of the executives we interviewed gave Ford cars of Europe as an example of the differences observed in consumer perceptions. Bovée and Arens (27) suggest similar variations in consumer attitudes to car ownership from one culture to another, even if the product remains the same. In the almost classless Scandinavian countries, cars are seen as functional vehicles that have no luxury values. In underdeveloped countries, however, cars are a symbol of wealth and position, as they are owned, in the main, by government officials and bureaucrats. Under such conditions, it is extremely difficult to run international campaigns.

D. Danbar of JWT referred to another study (28) that shows that, out of the 31 countries surveyed, 9 imposed an effective ban on TV and radio material produced by and for other nations; 5 required some changes; and a further 5, through technical or financial regulations, made it unusually time-consuming and costly to use imported material. Only 12 of the 31 countries did not create obstacles.

Although 'cost saving' is usually cited as the main advantage of international advertising, some of the account executives we interviewed had reservations even about this. Global campaigns require more co-ordination and more consultation with senior people. Thinking the campaign through and selling it to individual local operations can take a long time. Companies can easily outspend any gains they may have made. Executives who had doubts about global advertising therefore regarded the pan-European approach to be more acceptable. Twenty years or so ago, Miracle (16) cited advertising legislation as a restriction to international advertising. However, such restrictions are now incorporated into creative briefs and, though there still are major barriers that need to be lifted for the successful transfer of international campaigns, advertising legislation is far less persistent and perplexing than the low morale of local creatives or the issue of local-agency commissions (see Chapter 8).

MATCHING ADVERTISING TYPE TO THE GLOBAL CAMPAIGN

The executives we interviewed generally favoured advertising types that had emotional appeal, showed life styles and product features and were visual, simple and factual, relying less on language, pun and humour. Dunn and Barban (29) complement these findings when they cite Scott Paper Co. as having standardised its advertising successfully by the use of strong visuals, sound and music rather than lengthy dialogues.

STANDARDISING MARKETING MIX

Table 10.2 summarises the three main groups of marketing-mix elements and the degree to which they must be standardised for the successful transfer of the campaigns described in this book. The agencies generally emphasised the standardisation of those elements that directly affect a campaign's creative development (product positioning, consumer target group and end-use application), and put less emphasis on those elements they are only minimally involved in and about which they may have little information (e.g. pricing and distribution).

TRAPS TO AVOID WHEN MEASURING 'SUCCESSFUL' ADVERTISING

The use of sales as a measure of a campaign's success was still very widespread in the agencies studied (see Chapter 8). Although somewhat sceptical about it, 9% of agency executives suggested creative excellence as another measure. Agencies invariably set advertising objectives before the start of a campaign, but in 33% of cases they did not refer back to these. The use of the DAGMAR model also seemed to be rather restricted. On the whole, agency executives seemed to rely on intangible measures, such as whether or not the client liked it, what other peer groups thought about it or whether or not it made its presence felt in sales charts.

HOW SUCCESSFUL GLOBAL CAMPAIGNS COME TO LIFE

As shown in Chapter 9, the lead-agency method was, by far, the most common method employed on the 39 accounts included in this book, appearing at all points on the decentralisation–centralisation continuum. The second approach was the 'collaborative approach', where all an agency's resources pulled together to create a campaign to a global brief, each office developing its own idea. This approach seems to be gaining popularity, as more and more clients move towards centralised advertising, especially pan-European (for example, the International Wool Secretariat's 'Love from Woolmark' pan-European press and magazine campaign, launched in February 1989 and produced by CLM: BBDO (the French subsidiary of BBDO), to be used in 16 European countries

Table 10.2 The marketing-mix elements of successfully, transferred campaigns and the degree of standardisation applied

Standardisation	Total	High	Moderate	Low
	Crucial elements	Supplementary elements	Marginal elements	
Marketing-Mix Elements	Product positioning	Brand name	Pack sizes	Market shares
	Consumer target group	Package type	Product life-cycle	Competitors and expenditures
	End-use application	Package aesthetics Label Available media Media types used Pricing structure	Advertising legislation	Distribution channels Role of retailers Type of retailers Role of sales force Management of sales force

in 12 different languages (30)). Another pan-regional advertisement was produced early in 1990 by Ajans Ada in Turkey, for Gillette Contour, to be used in Gillette International's Africa, Middle East, India and Eastern Europe (AMEE) region (covering 15 countries). The ad was shot with the help of computer animation. Two actors were used, a black actor being preferred for African countries (31). Griffin (32) has also emphasised the increasing popularity in the 1990s of regional campaigns as opposed to global ones.

The third approach was the American Express model. The US-originated campaign was shown in seven European countries, each country selecting the vignettes that would best suit their own market. Subsequently, new vignettes were shot for the whole of Europe. Production was realised in London, using the same set but changing the actors for each market. Post-production was left to local markets. It was also decided that, in future commercials, each local market would take turns in handling centralised production. This avoided the problem of low morale in local executives and put an end to the monopolisation of campaign production by a few resourceful countries. Local offices' budgeted incomes were thus not adversely affected.

Jereski (12) – referring to J. Deret, Marketing Manager for S. C. Johnson, Paris – suggests that one solution Deret offers to this problem is for a company to restructure itself into a system of lead countries, each country being responsible for the development and strategy of a product it knows well (hence again avoiding low morale). This is similar to the American Express solution. However, in the American Express solution, countries are assigned different campaigns rather than advertising different services. Peebles and Ryans (33) suggest a central group that could pool talent (the 'collaborative approach' and, more particularly, the American Express approach accord with this idea). The American Express solution, especially, bridges the gap between academic and practical approaches. Killough (19) recommends the setting up of a global creative team to develop advertising that consciously avoids or minimises the barriers to successful transfers. These barriers may be cultural, communicative, legislative, competitive and/or executional ones. Although these suggestions resemble those put forward in the American Express approach, Killough (*ibid.*) does not offer any explanation of how to achieve this.

FIRST UNDERSTAND YOUR CLIENT'S CORPORATE CULTURE

The interviews revealed that the way agencies developed campaigns actually reflected the client's corporate culture (campaigns for decentralised clients were less planned, less systematic, etc.). Campaign types and clients' corporate cultures were explained in Chapter 9 and summarised in Table 9.1.) By looking at the style adopted for a global advertisement, it is possible to locate a client's position on the decentralised–centralised continuum. Once the client's position is known, the agency can tackle the client in the most effective manner.

HOW FAR SHOULD A GLOBAL CAMPAIGN BE ADAPTED?

The results of the study show that, in successfully transferred international campaigns, the degree of adaptation should be kept to a minimum, generally to save production costs. The most common changes were to the music track or the voice-over (see Chapter 9), and those ads that were the most successful generally used non-verbal communication with a wide variety of visual aids. Although Almaney (34) and Hall (35) draw attention to the importance of non-verbal communication, Hecker and Stewart (36) point out that non-verbal communication includes how something is said, facial expressions, body movement, gestures, spacing, eye movement, pictures and symbolic artefacts. They also suggest that the use of imagery, visual aids, drawings, paintings, models, visual-memory devices, product, corporate symbols and music are all-pervasive in advertising.

A FINAL WARNING ABOUT SATELLITE TV

Although most of the account executives we interviewed considered the future of satellite TV to be promising, they also agreed that it is in its infancy and is only received by a minority. Before satellite is even considered, brands needed uniform communications – the same message, consumer group, usage and product positioning, etc. It therefore required plenty of preparation. Peebles (18) gives Nestlé as a courageous example for advertising on Sky Channel, emphasising the fact that Nestlé sells the same products in different packages and under different trade names throughout Europe. Another piece of research conducted by Howard and Ryans (37) analyses advertisers' and agencies' views about satellite TV. They point out that advertisers and agencies both agree strongly that satellite TV will have a profound effect on advertising in Europe, which supports the findings reported in this book (see Chapter 9). Both agencies and advertisers also mention a significant increase in HQ control over local markets' advertising activities. A growing emphasis on the visual aspects of communication in future international advertising is also stressed. It is believed that these messages will attempt to reflect European similarities rather than differences. Although Howard and Ryans' research was conducted on European members of the International Advertising Association, their results greatly resemble our own. They also conclude that satellite TV is a significant medium that has already been recognised, particularly by agencies.

TAKING IT UP FROM HERE ...

It is hoped that, by now, the questions posed at the end of Chapter 5 have, to a great extent, been answered. While I do not in any way assert that this is a perfect piece of research, I hope that readers will have found something worth while in it. My wish is that this book will be seen as a stepping-stone in the area of global advertising. The same research could have been conducted on service industries, looking at the transfer of campaigns all over Europe; there is a similar lack of research on industrial products.

The results obtained here reflect the perceptions and, to some extent, the prejudices of local-branch management teams. As was shown in Chapter 5, depending on where the study was conducted (whether it was at HQ or in the subsidiary country), the degrees of HQ involvement reported changed. As an extension to this study, therefore, it would be interesting to interview executives in agencies' actual HOs and regional HOs as the branches that create campaigns for corresponding brands. UK lead-agency and regional HO executives' responses could be compared. It might thus be possible to see whether agency HOs exaggerate their own power and if local agency branches under-estimate the extent of the involvement they receive from their lead agencies or regional HOs. We also believe that, rather than registered (official) HOs, lead agencies and the regional HOs (or international co-ordination units) need to be researched thoroughly. The roles of regional HOs do not appear to be understood by local agency branches. The hostile feelings held by local agency executives could be dispelled if these co-ordination bodies' roles were understood better.

The book closes with a checklist for practitioners to use as a tool to assist them in their campaign-transfer decisions. It is addressed directly to agency executives and is called the 'magic checklist' for marketing purposes!

THE MAGIC CHECKLIST

The following checklist is drawn from the entire research findings included in this book and aims to be action-orientated. In our opinion, each affirmative answer to the thirty questions advances an account closer to successful global transfer. It is free of jargon and, it is hoped, makes realistic recommendations.

1. Do you reflect meticulously your international client's organisation within your own?
2. Do you restructure your account management team each time an organisational change takes place within your client?
3. Does your client find his or her exact counterpart in each market?
4. Does your client's HQ have a 'high' level of involvement in its affiliates' marketing activities, including advertising?
5. Does the client's HQ have its affiliates' loyalty and moral support for running global campaigns?
6. Does the client's HQ have line authority over its affiliate companies?
7. Is the same or similar brand produced and marketed by the client's HQ?
8. Is this brand's counterpart in your client's home country promoted by your own HO?
9. Is your lead agency on this specific account close to the client's HQ?
10. Does your client insist on global marketing/advertising?

11. If you are transferring a campaign to other local agency offices, are these local branches relatively smaller offices within the network?
12. Do you think global advertising is very difficult to implement?
13. Are you aware of some less evident problems of global advertising (such as low morale among local creatives, difficulties in splitting up production costs, difficulties in agency commissions)?
14. Are you aware that some of the widely cited advantages of global advertising (such as cost savings) can be cancelled out rather easily?
15. Does your brand belong to any of these groupings?

    - youth products?
    - fashion products (latest trends)?
    - homogeneous products?
    - status-symbol brands for cosmopolitan consumers?

16. Does your brand have similar or the same

    - product positioning?
    - consumer target group?
    - end-use application?

    as its counterpart, with which an exchange of advertising campaign is likely?
17. Is the specific campaign to be transferred based on

    - an emotional-appeal type of advertising (showing different life-styles/vignettes)?
    - emphasising 'product features'?
    - stressing 'visual aid'?

18. Is it visual, simple, factual, and free of subtlety, humour or puns?
19. Does it deal with extrinsics rather than intrinsics?
20. Do you know why it was successful in the other countries in which it was run?
21. Are many local offices involved in the campaign's preproduction stages?
22. Will this campaign transfer motivate local agency offices?
23. Is 'local sensitivity' being incorporated while the campaign is being centrally executed?
24. Will you be able to take part in a well-co-ordinated, organised, collaborative task with other agency offices?
25. Are the procedures for new-campaign development well established by the client and your agency? Are they precise and coherent enough?
26. Have you had any previous global advertising activities in your account?
27. Was this specific campaign designed intentionally to be a global campaign? Was it developed to a global brief?
28. Can you run this same campaign for your brand without making any drastic adaptations?
29. Will you consider advertising this brand on one of the satellite TV channels?

30. Have you and your client already started making preparations for 1992?

This checklist may also be useful in assessing a brand's readiness for 1992. Until now it has been very much to the discretion of an individual company whether or not it mounted an international campaign. However, that freedom will soon be regulated and shaped by the EEC's efforts to harmonise Europe. In addition, developments taking place in China, in the Soviet Union and in other East European countries should be evaluated. Soviet television started commercial advertising in May 1988 with Ford, Pepsi Cola and Sony ads. Hungary's first commercial TV channel – Mtv Plusz – was also launched in May 1988. All these signs suggest that global advertising is here to stay, and agencies and advertisers need to be fully equipped to meet the challenges.

We wish to end the book with a quotation from Bertrand Russell. In our opinion, it readily applies to global advertising, which cries out for rhyme or reason:

> The matters in which the interest of nations are supposed to clash are mainly three: tariffs which are a delusion; the exploitation of inferior races which is a crime; pride of power and dominion, which is a schoolboy folly.
>
> While this temper persists, the hope of international co-operation must remain dim.
>
> (*Political Ideas*, 1963, p. 71–3)

REFERENCES

1. Elinder, E. (1965) How international can European advertising be? *Journal of Marketing*, Vol. 29, April, pp. 7–11.
2. Jugenheimer, D. W. (1976) Forecast for future advertising strategies, in R. D. Michman and D. W. Jugenheimer (eds.) *Strategic Advertising Decisions: Selected Readings*, Grid Publications, Columbus, Ohio, pp. 411–5.
3. Miracle, G. E. (1966) *The Role of Advertising Agencies: Management of International Advertising*, Michigan International Studies, Michigan, no. 5.
4. Advertising: Europe's new Common Market (1984) *Business Week*, 23 July, pp. 62–5.
5. O'Connor, J. (1979) International advertising, in S. W. Dunn and E. S. Lorimor (eds.) *International Advertising and Marketing*, Grid Publications, Columbus, Ohio, pp. 69–78 (first published in *Journal of Advertising*, Vol. 3, no. 2. Spring, 1974, pp. 9–14).
6. McCann-Erickson in Europe (agency report, courtesy of McCann-Erickson).
7. Terpstra, V. and Yu, C. M. (1988) Determinants of foreign investment of US advertising agencies, *Journal of International Business Studies*, Spring, pp. 33–46.
8. Aydin, N., Terpstra, V. and Yaprak, A. (1984) The American challenge in international advertising, *Journal of Advertising*, Fall, pp. 49–57.
9. Pocklington, K. (1987) The good business of project billing (paper presented at the Fifteenth World Industrial Advertising Congress), Brussels.
10. Jivani, A. (1985) Where global obstacles lie, *Marketing*, 4 July, pp. 20–6.
11. Gardner, F. (1984) BBDO thinks beyond just global options, *Marketing and Media Decisions*, December, pp. 52, 53, 133.
12. Jereski, L. K. (1984) Foote Cone lets the client lead, *Marketing and Media Decisions*, December, pp. 54, 134, 135.
13. Gerrie, A. (1987) Ads sans frontieres, *Marketing*, 2 April, pp. 43–4.

14. Taking a long, hard look at where global marketing's going (1984) *Marketing and Media Decisions*, December, pp. 34–8, 40, 42, 108, 110, 112, 114, 116, 117, 126.
15. Roostal, I. (1963) Standardization of advertising for Western Europe, *Journal of Marketing*, Vol. 27, October, pp. 15–20.
16. Miracle, G. (1968) International advertising principles and strategies, *MSU Business Topics*, Vol. 16, Fall, pp. 29–36.
17. Naylor, L., (1987) Managing decentralised accounts (presentation given at the Ogilvy & Mather Worldwide Accounts Seminar), Troutbeck, July (courtesy of O & M).
18. Peebles, D. M. (1989) Executive insights, don't write off global advertising: a commentary, *International Marketing Review*, Vol. 6, no. 1, pp. 73–8.
19. Killough, J. (1978) Improved Payoffs from transnational advertising, *Harvard Business Review*, July/August, pp. 102–10.
20. Wiechmann, U. E. and Pringle, L. G. (1979) Problems that plague multinational marketers, *Harvard Business Review*, July/August, pp. 118–24.
21. Peebles, D. M. and Ryans, J. K. jr (1984) *Management of International Advertising – A Marketing Approach*, Allyn & Bacon, Boston, Mass.
22. Gilligan, C. and Hird, M. (1986) *International Marketing: Strategy and Management*, Croom Helm, London.
23. Bernstein, D. (1984) *Company Image and Reality*, Holt, Rinehart & Winston/The Advertising Association, Eastbourne.
24. Daniels, J. D. (1987) Bridging national and global marketing strategies through regional operations, *International Marketing Review*, Autumn, pp. 29–44.
25. Vardar, N. and Paliwoda, S. J. (1989) International advertising agencies' organisational structure for global campaigns ('The Mirroring Effect') (Marketing Education Group Proceedings of the Twenty-Second Annual Conference), in L. Moutinho, D. Brownlie and J. Livingstone (eds.) *Marketing Audit of the 80s*, Glasgow Business School, Vol. I, 11–14 July, pp. 425–52.
26. Rijkens, R. (1972) International campaigns – a fallacy? *The International Advertiser*, Vol. 13, no. 2, pp. 7–9, 20.
27. Bovée, C. L. and Arens, W. F. (1986) *Contemporary Advertising*, (2nd edn), Irwin, Homewood, Ill.
28. Boddewyn, J. J. (1987) International advertisers face government hurdles, *Marketing News*, 8 May, pp. 20–1, 26.
29. Dunn, S. W. and Barban, A. W. (1986) *Advertising: Its Role in Modern Marketing* (6th edn) CBS College Publishing, New York, NY.
30. Rawsthorn, A. (1989) Turning people on to wool, *The Financial Times*, 26 January.
31. Ajans Ada'nın Dünya Pazarı Için Ilk filmi (1990) *Medya*, Volume 3, no. 5, April, p. 1 (in Turkish).
32. Griffin, T. (1985) International Advertising in the 1990s, in S. Shaw, L. Sparks and E. Kaynak (eds.) *Marketing in the 1990s and Beyond* (Second World Marketing Congress Proceedings), Marketing Education Group, 28–31 August, University of Stirling, Vol. II, pp. 622–31.
33. Peebles, D. M. and Ryans, J. K. jr (1983) One international cultural philosophy, *International Advertiser*, Part II, January/February, pp. 16–18.
34. Almaney, A. (1974) Intercultural communication and the multinational company executive, *Columbia Journal of World Business*, Winter, pp. 23–8.
35. Hall, E. T. (1960) The silent language in overseas business, *Harvard Business Review*, Vol. 38, no. 3 May/June, pp. 87–96.
36. Hecker, S. and Stewart, D. W. (1988) *Nonverbal Communication in Advertising*, Heath, Lexington, Mass.
37. Howard, D. G. and Ryans, J. K. jr (1988/1989) The probable effect of satellite TV on agency/client relationships, *Journal of Advertising Research*, December/January, pp. 41–6.

APPENDIX I
HOW THE RESEARCH WAS CONDUCTED

DEFINING THE SAMPLE OF AGENCIES

The main objective of this research was to examine agency head office (AHO) involvement in the UK offices of international advertising agencies when running successfully transferable global campaigns. More specifically, the intention was to discover those certain prerequisites necessary for local agency branches to ensure smooth campaign transfers. Where possible, international advertising agencies operating in the UK but whose head offices (HOs) were located in other countries were chosen (the test-bed of the research). However, the number of agencies that fell into this category was rather limited, and so it was decided to gather data through personally administered interviews. (It was also thought that face-to-face interviews would help to achieve a better understanding of the subject.)

SELECTING THE AGENCIES

When selecting the agency sample, *Who Owns Whom* (1) was examined (under industry code 83), as well as *Jordan's Britain's Top 1,000 Foreign Owned Companies* (2), *Advertising Age Yearbook* (3) and *KOMPASS* (4) (under code 81.20). The agencies selected were then checked with *Key British Enterprises 1987* (5) to find out where their HOs were based (telephone numbers and addresses were also obtained from this source). The agencies' current client lists were taken from *Advertisers & Agency List* (6, 7) in order to ascertain their specific international clients. This directory was also used to find names for the initial contact letter. Selection was completed by November 1987. A total of 31 agencies were identified as suitable for contact. All were advertising agencies with international networks, and all (except 8) had HOs outside the UK. The respondents chosen were the account executives or account directors who were responsible for international brands (in charge of the account's advertising and its management). Their responsibilities were wide ranging, from day-to-day tasks to determining annual advertising objectives in consultation with the client's brand managers.

The initial letters were sent to the publicity managers (or promotions managers) of the 31 agencies, and this asked for the names of those account executives who handled international consumer non-durable goods and/or service accounts. This letter also asked for the agencies' co-operation in the research and requested their permission to include them. However, when the agencies were subsequently contacted by telephone to obtain these names, it was found that most did not have a publicity manager (only 4, in fact, had publicity or promotions managers). After this false start, the same contact letter was sent to chief executive officer (CEO) positions (for example, chairman, director, regional managing director and international new business director).

Subsequent telephone contact with CEOs revealed that, of the 31 earlier-identified agencies, only 13 were suitable for our study (5 did not want to participate and the remaining 13 were not appropriate as they were specialist agencies or they did not have international clients). The 13 selected were all based in London. Overall, 30 account executives, account managers, account supervisors, account directors and international account co-ordinators were interviewed (comprising 36 international accounts from 12 agencies). The thirteenth agency was Saatchi & Saatchi (S & S), who did not agree to be interviewed. Instead they offered to complete postal questionnaires (see Appendix II). These questionnaires were sent to S & S's Promotions Manager for distribution to three of their account executives. In addition, two S & S affiliates (DFS Dorland and Ted Bates) were included in the study, but this time the data was collected from these two agencies by personal interviews. (These two agencies had not been merged at the time of the interviews.) Another UK-based agency included in the sample was Lowe Howard-Spink (LHS). LHS was an affiliate of Interpublic until the beginning of 1986. At that time, Lowe was trying to establish for itself an international network and therefore agreed to buy the Campbell-Ewald network from Interpublic. Thus, although LHS was a UK-owned agency, it had an international network and a certain degree of contact with Interpublic, mainly because of historical ties. The last UK agency was J. Walter Thompson (JWT). JWT was acquired by UK-based WPP in May 1987, but the New York office was still considered to be the actual HO. This was WPP's particular wish at the time, so that the agency and its clients would not suffer any organisational changes. (As the agency interviews were complete by June 1988, Ogilvy & Mather (O & M) had as yet not been acquired by WPP.)

CONTACTING THE INTERVIEWEES

Once account executives' names had been obtained, the same contact letter was sent to them to outline the project. They were subsequently telephoned to see whether or not they would be able to take part in the research and, if so, when (the major obstacle in collecting agency data). The account executives had very tight schedules, and eight weeks was spent in trying to obtain agency contacts before dates could be fixed for the actual interviews. Each agency was telephoned, on average, seven or eight times before an appointment could be arranged. In addition, job turnover rates were very high, and a constant organisational restructuring was taking place within the agencies contacted. During the period of the interviews, two agencies merged and another was dissolved and renamed (and two account executives left their agencies).

The interviews started in March 1988. They were conducted throughout May and were completed by June 1988 (including the three postal questionnaires sent to S & S). All the agencies were co-operative and genuinely interested in the project; once appointments were fixed and confirmed, they were willing and helpful. Overall:

- 30 people were interviewed in 12 agencies, which produced information about 36 international accounts;
- S & S contributed through 3 completed postal questionnaires;
- 13 agencies were included, obtaining 33 contacts and covering 39 international accounts; and
- 8 of the 13 agencies had their HOs in the USA, the remaining 5 being UK-owned.

The interviews lasted from half an hour to two hours, but on average took over one hour. Of the 30 interviewees, 21 were asked whether or not they would mind being tape-recorded: no one refused.

THE QUESTIONNAIRE

Before the agency questionnaire was devised, pilot contacts were made with two different practitioners. These contacts were used to ascertain the correct questions to ask the account executives. One contact was a partner in and the Director of a national agency based in Manchester that also had other UK branches. Although a national agency, it had freelance copywriters and creatives in other countries who would deal with international requests as they arose. The second contact was an account planner in Young & Rubicam (Y & R), who was particularly useful in shaping the questionnaire and in forming research objectives. After these discussions, the agency questionnaire was devised. When actual data collection started in March 1988, the first two personal interviews were also considered as pilot studies. As information was gathered, the questionnaire was used mostly as a detailed checklist (see Appendix II for the questionnaire used in the personal interviews). As each account was slightly different from the others, small modifications were made to accommodate individual specifications. In addition, some of the points raised in earlier agency interviews were mentioned in subsequent interviews with other account people to check whether or not the points were true in general or specific to a particular account or agency.

The second version of the questionnaire was the postal one for S & S. This was similar in content to the other questionnaire, but the questions had been rephrased as the respondents were based at the agency's HO itself.

SUMMARY TABLES OF AGENCY PROFILES

Of the agencies in the sample, four were represented by one account executive. However, the arithmetic mean of the personal interviews held with each agency was between 2–3 (30/12 = 2.5). The number of interviews that were conducted depended mainly upon the number of international clients the agency had, as well as how sensitive its clients were about discussing their advertising activities with third parties. In some cases, more than one account was discussed with the same account executive. Therefore, the number of accounts (39) included in the research exceeds the total number of contacts (33) obtained from the 13 agencies. The number of account executives interviewed in each agency is given in Table AI.1.

The sectors covered in the sample were drinks, food, toiletries & cosmetics, airlines, office equipment, batteries, toys, electrical appliances, photographic films, cigarettes, petrol, stationery, cars and credit cards. The most heavily represented sectors were drinks, toiletries & cosmetics, food and airlines.

A list of the agencies included in the research is given in Table AI.2, together with their annual billings and the number of their employees. The figures were obtained from the interviewees and updated according to BRAD (8).

The mean of agencies' annual billings was £130 million, the range being between £16 million and £340 million. Five of the agencies included in the sample had annual billings that were above average. The average number of employees was 330. The smallest agency had 40 people and the largest 800. Harrison Interpublic had the lowest annual billings and the least number of employees; S & S had the highest annual billings and the most number of employees.

Media expenditures for the accounts in 1987 were obtained from MEAL (9). Expen-

Table AI.1 Number of interviewees and accounts covered in the agency sample

Advertising agency	No. of interviewees (no. of accounts)
BBDO	4 (4)
DDB Needham	1 (1)
Dorland	1 (1)
Foote Cone & Belding	1 (1)
Harrison Interpublic	2 (3)
J. Walter Thompson	2 (4)
Leo Burnett	3 (3)
Lowe Howard-Spink	1 (1)
McCann-Erickson Int.	5 (5)
Ogilvy & Mather	4 (4)
Saatchi & Saatchi	3 (3)*
Ted Bates	2 (3)
Young & Rubicam	4 (6)
Total number (13)	33 (39)

Note
* Data gathered through postal questionnaires.

Table AI.2 The agencies contacted, their annual billings and the number of their employees

Agency	Annual billings (£m)†	No. of employees†
1. BBDO	65	83
2. DDB Needham	50	135
3. Dorland*	190	589
4. Foote Cone & Belding	71	300
5. Harrison Interpublic	16	40
6. J. Walter Thompson	222	550
7. Leo Burnett	77	220
8. Lowe Howard-Spink	120	252
9. McCann-Erickson Int.	112	320
10. Ogilvy & Mather	146	356
11. Saatchi & Saatchi	340	800
12. Ted Bates*	100	250
13. Young & Rubicam	154	370

Notes
* Interviews conducted before the two agencies merged in May 1988.
† According to BRAD, October 1988 (Reference 8).

ditures varied from as low as £130,000 to £8.7 million. The mean value was £2.45 million, with a mode value of between £1.10 million and £1.90 million. This information was not requested from agency executives as it was available from secondary sources.

The most commonly used media type in the accounts included in the study was, according to MEAL (9), TV. Only 8 accounts were cited as using press predominantly over other media types (this clear preference for TV airing also being apparent in our sample group).

REFERENCES

1. *Who Owns Whom* (1987) (UK and Republic of Ireland), Vol. I, Dun & Bradstreet, London.
2. *Jordan's Britain's Top 1000 Foreign Owned Companies* (1982) Jordan & Sons, Bristol.
3. *Advertising Age Yearbook* (1984) Crain Books, Chicago.
4. *KOMPASS* (1987) (in association with the Confederation of British Industry Products and Services), Vols. I and II, East Grinstead.
5. *Key British Enterprises 1987* (1987/1988) (Britain's top 20,000 companies), Vols. I and II, Dun & Bradstreet, London.
6. *Advertisers and Agency List* (1987) British Rate and Data (BRAD) Publications, London, October.
7. *Advertisers and Agency List* (1988) British Rate and Data (BRAD) Publications, London, January.
8. *Advertisers and Agency List* (1988) British Rate and Data (BRAD) Publications, London, October.
9. *Tri-Media Digest of Brands and Advertisers and Advertiser Index* (1987) Media Expenditure Analysis Ltd (MEAL) London, fourth quarter.

APPENDIX II
AGENCY QUESTIONNAIRES USED IN DATA COLLECTION

VERSION USED IN PERSONAL INTERVIEWS

Agency Profile

Name of the UK advertising agency:
....
Your agency's annual turnover:
....
No. of employees in the UK:
....
Name of the parent company:
....
Home country of the parent company:
....

1. HO Involvement in Advertising Campaign Decisions and the Extent of Advertising Standardisation Employed by the HO

1.1 How would you express your HO involvement in your account's advertising activities?

- High involvement
- Always involved in broad terms
- Head office is usually informed of our activities
- We sometimes seek their advice
- Practically no involvement

1.2 What is the extent of your HO involvement in your accounts?

- Always/usually/in exceptional cases the same accounts
- Explicit/implicit agreement with HO on accounts
- MR Guidelines sent by the HO

- Charging the same per cent of commission as the HO
- Transfer of advertising campaigns from the HO

1.3 In general what are your feelings about the transferability of advertising campaigns from HO to affiliates?

- Totally for it
- Does not cause problems
- No idea
- Very hard to implement
- Totally against it

1.4 What type of advertising do you think is easier to transfer from HO to affiliates?

- Product features/demonstration
- Customer needs
- Emotional appeal
- Testimonials
- Side-by-side comparisons/blind product tests
- Comparisons with competitors' products
- Stressed visual aid

1.5 How can you compare the brand you are promoting in the UK with its counterpart being promoted by your HO agency?
What is the degree of standardisation or differentiation applied to your account on the points mentioned below?

Packaging and marketing elements *Degree of standardisation/differentiation*

(a) *Packaging elements*
- Label (instructions, units)
- Package type
- Package aesthetics
- Pack sizes

(b) *Brand personality*
- Brand name
- Product positioning
- Consumer target group
- End-use application/prod. usage patterns
- Brand relaunches: stage on PLC
- Targeted market shares

(c) *Advertising environment*
- Media available
- Media types used
- Advertising legislation
- Competitors and their expenditures

(d) *Other marketing-mix elements*
- Distribution channels
- Pricing
- Type and role of retailer
- Role of sales force
- Management of sales force

2. Defining 'Successful' Advertising

2.1 How do you generally define 'successful' advertising campaigns?

2.2 Who sets the advertising objectives for each campaign before you start the campaign?

- Advertisers' marketing departments – PMs
- Clients' HQs
- Advertising agency – account executives
- Agency's HO
- No objectives are set

2.3 Do you generally measure the success of your advertising campaign against the predetermined advertising objectives?

- Is this the general practice or an exceptional case?

3. Specific Successful Global Campaign

Now please think of a successful advertising campaign conducted for one of your international accounts that was recommended to you by your HO.

There is no time limit. It could date back or could be a very recent one.

3.1 Could you summarise the specifics of this advertising campaign?
What was it about?

- Timing
- Duration
- Any repeats
- Type of advertising
- Kind of campaign

3.2 Who has originally produced this campaign?

- Your HO
- Another affiliate of your agency
  Which one?______
- Client (UK)
- Client's HQ

3.3 What was the advertising objective of this specific advertising campaign which you consider to be successful?

3.4 To what extent did this successful advertising campaign fulfil its predetermined advertising objectives?

3.5 Why was this campaign recommended to you by your HO?

- Successful at the home country of the HO
- Successful in other affiliates

- Prototype campaign for all affiliates
- HO always sends – the general practice
- Global advertising
- Advertising costs
- Simplifying subsidiary tasks

3.6 (a) Did you use this campaign as it was recommended to you by your HO?
(b) Did you make any amendments – adaptations?

3.7 What were the adaptations you made? Could you describe them?

3.8 Who actually made the decision for these adaptations?

- You, as the UK advertising agency?
- You, after consulting your HO?
- You, following HO approval?
- Your HO?
- Your HO, after consulting you?
- Your UK client?
- UK client's HQ?

3.9 Was this campaign used by

- Your HO?
- Another affiliate of your agency?
  Which one?______

Please mention the 'pack design–brand name' mix used for the campaign as it was employed by the HO and/or affiliates.
Was it successful as it was used at the HO and/or in any other affiliate?

3.10 Which of the elements of this advertising campaign have you, as the UK advertising agency, actually adapted to the UK market? What was the degree of adaptation?

Advertising elements adapted *Degree of adaptation*

3.11 Taking into consideration the latest developments in the media, how do you see the future of global advertising, especially in Europe? How will the 'new media' affect HO involvement in your accounts?

POSTAL VERSION OF THE QUESTIONNAIRE

Agency Profile

Name of the UK advertising agency:

....

Your agency's annual turnover:

....

No. of employees in the UK:

....

1. HO Involvement in Advertising Campaign Decisions and the Extent of Advertising Standardisation Employed by the HO

1.1 How would you express your involvement as the HO in your international accounts' advertising activities?

High involvement in every respect	Always involved in broad terms	HO is usually informed of their activities	Our advice as the HO is sometimes asked	Practically no involvement

1.2 What is the extent of your involvement in your international accounts? (In other words, do you expect them to have the same accounts? Is there any explicit/implicit agreement on which accounts they can take on?
Do your non-UK affiliates charge the same per cent of commission as the HO?
Do you send market research guidelines to your affiliates?
Do you regularly transfer advertising campaigns to your affiliates?)

1.3 In general what are your feelings about transferability of advertising campaigns from HO to affiliates?

Totally for it	Usually does not cause any problems	No idea	Very hard to implement	Totally against it

1.4 What type of advertising do you think is easier to transfer from HO to affiliates? (You may circle more than one answer.)

- Product features/demonstration
- Customer needs
- Emotional appeal
- Testimonials
- Side-by-side comparisons/blind product tests
- Comparisons with competitors' products
- Stressed visual aid

1.5 Generally speaking, how can you compare brands you are promoting in the HO with their counterparts being promoted by your non-UK affiliates?

What is the degree of standardisation or differentiation applied to your accounts on the points mentioned below.

Packaging and marketing elements	*Degree of standardisation/ differentiation (in percentages)*
(a) *Packaging elements*	
• Label (instruction, units)	
• Package type	
• Package aesthetics	
• Pack sizes	
(b) *Brand personality*	
• Brand name	
• Product positioning	
• Consumer target group	
• End-use application/prod. usage patterns	
• Brand relaunches; stage on PLC	
• Targeted market shares	
(c) *Advertising environment*	
• Media available	
• Media types used	
• Advertising legislation	
• Competitors and their expenditures	
(d) *Other marketing-mix elements*	
• Distribution channels	
• Pricing	
• Type and role of retailer	
• Role of sales force	
• Management of sales force	

2. Defining 'Successful' Advertising

2.1 How do you generally define 'successful' advertising campaigns?

2.2 What are the preconditions that enable successful transfer of advertising across borders?

2.3 Who sets the advertising objectives for each campaign before you start a global campaign? Is there a certain pattern?

- Advertisers' marketing departments – PMs (in each country)
- Clients' HQs
- Your affiliated agency in each country

- You, as the HO
- No objectives are set

2.4 Do you generally measure the success of your advertising campaign against the predetermined advertising objectives?

- Is this the general practice or an exceptional case?

3. Specific Successful Global Campaign

Now please think of a successful global advertising campaign conducted for one of your international accounts that was transferred from the HO to one of your non-UK affiliates.

There is no time limit. It could date back or could be a very recent one.

3.1 Could you summarise the specifics of this advertising campaign? What was it about?
- Place (which affiliate it was transferred to?)
- Timing
- Duration
- Any repeats
- Type of advertising (press, TV, radio, etc.)
- Kind of campaign (basic thematic, specific consumer camp., launch of a product, relaunch, new-package/pack-size announcement, etc.)

3.2 Who originally produced this campaign?

- You as the HO?
- Another affiliate of your agency?
  Which one?______

3.3 What was the advertising objective of this specific advertising campaign which you consider to be successful?

3.4 To what extent did this successful advertising campaign fulfil its predetermined advertising objectives in that non-UK affiliate's country?

3.5 Why did you recommend this campaign to your non-UK affiliate?

- Successful here at the HO
- Successful in other affiliates
- Prototype campaign for all affiliates
- HO always sends – it is the general practice
- For practising global advertising
- For attaining economies of scale in advertising costs
- For simplifying subsidiary tasks

Any other reasons?

3.6 (a) Did they use this campaign as it was recommended to them by you? Yes/No.
(b) Did they make any amendments – adaptations? Yes/No.

3.7 What were the adaptations they have made? Could you describe them?

3.8 Who actually made the decision for these adaptations?

- You as the HO?

- Your non-UK affiliate agency, by itself?
- Your non-UK affiliate following your approval?
- Your non-UK affiliate after consulting you?
- You, after consulting your non-UK affiliate?
- Your client in the UK?
- Your client's HQ?

3.9 Was this campaign used by

- You – the HO?
- Another affiliate of your agency? (other than the one already mentioned) Which one?______

How would you compare the 'pack design–brand name' mix used for the campaign by your non-UK affiliate and the HO or other affiliates?
Was the pack design the same or different?
Was the brand name the same or different?
Please circle the correct 'pack design–brand name' mix on the chart given below:

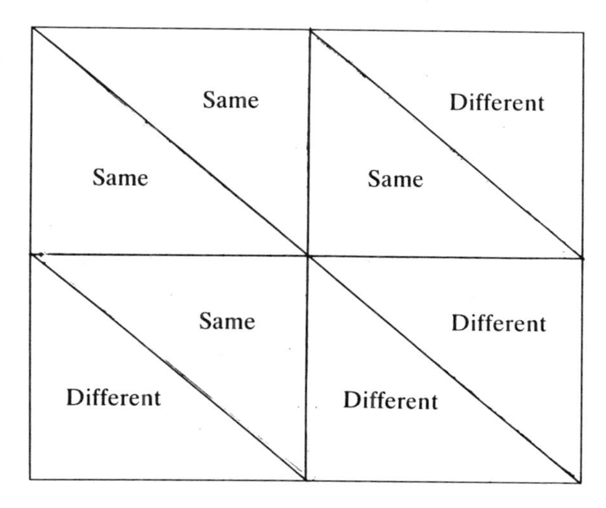

Was it a success as it was used? Yes/No.

3.10 Which of the following elements of this advertising campaign was actually adapted to your non-UK affiliate's market? What was the degree of adaptation (in percentages please)?

Advertising elements adapted	*Degree of adaptation*
• Pictorial images/graphics/ photos/illustrations	
• Layout	
• Copy	
• Jingle	
• Typography	
• Choice of colour(s)	
• Dimension (POPs, press ads)	
• Length of commercial	
• Type and quality of materials used	
• Content – general theme	
• Execution	
• Translation/transliteration	

Others (please specify)

3.11 Taking into consideration the latest developments in the 'media', how do you see the future of global advertising, especially in Europe? How will the 'new media' affect HO involvement in your international accounts?

INDEX